TurboStrategy

21 Powerful Ways to Transform Your Business and Boost Your Profits Quickly

Brian Tracy

AMACOM

American Management Association

New York • Atlanta • Chicago • Kansas City • San Francisco • Washington, D. C.
Brussels • Toronto • Mexico City • Tokyo

Special discounts on bulk quantities of AMACOM books are available to corpora-
tions, professional associations, and other organizations. For details, contact Special
Sales Department, AMACOM, a division of American Management Association,
1601 Broadway, New York, NY 10019.
Tel.: 212-903-8316   Fax: 212-903-8083
Web site: www.amacombooks.org

This publication is designed to provide accurate and authoritative information in regard to
the subject matter covered. It is sold with the understanding that the publisher is not
engaged in rendering legal, accounting, or other professional service. If legal advice or
other expert assistance is required, the services of a competent professional person should
be sought.

Library of Congress Cataloging-in-Publication Data

Tracy, Brian.
  Turbostrategy : 21 powerful ways to transform your business and boost
your profits quickly / Brian Tracy.
      p. cm.
Includes bibliographical references and index.
  ISBN 0-8144-7193-5
  1. Strategic planning. 2. Reengineering (Management) I. Title.
HD30.28.T724 2003
  658.4'012—dc21   2003005128

Printing number
10 9 8 7 6 5 4 3 2 1

To Peter Drucker, the finest management thinker and business philosopher of this age or any age. Your insights, ideas, and observations have been a continuous source of knowledge and inspiration to me, for which I am continuously grateful.

Contents

Preface

Thank you for reading this book. In the pages ahead, I will show you how to turbocharge your business quickly, increasing sales and revenues, cutting costs and boosting profits by applying the best techniques and strategies ever discovered for operating a successful business, in any economy or under any competitive conditions.

You will quickly learn a series of practical, proven ideas, methods, and techniques used by all successful companies that survive and thrive in tough markets.

You will learn how to clarify the vision, values, mission, purpose, and goals of your company and how to use this increased clarity to achieve greater revenues and profitability in the months ahead.

To save you time and to help you get more and better results as quickly as possible, I'll give you ideas that have been distilled from years of experience and from hundreds of books and articles on strategy, planning, marketing, selling, and business success.

The most important part of this book, however, is not what you read or learn, but what you actually *do* with these practical, proven concepts. Action is everything. As you read, think about specific steps you can take immediately to apply these ideas in your business.

In business, as in so many areas of life, results are everything. As you go along, think about how these strategies can help you to get better results faster!

My Reasons for Writing This Book

My reasons for writing this book on Turbostrategy are twofold. First, I want to help you to be more successful in your business, whatever it is or wherever you find yourself in your career today.

My second reason for writing this book is that I want to introduce you to the practical techniques that you must master to survive and thrive in the increasingly turbulent and challenging business climate of the twenty-first century.

I call this approach *Turbostrategy* because it is an intensive, fast, focused, and effective way of setting and implementing strategy. It is for executives and companies that want to make immediate changes and get better results faster.

Consider the Consequences

There is a simple rule for setting priorities or determining the value of any decision or action: It revolves around the idea of *consequences*. An action or decision that is important is something that has significant potential consequences. The greater the potential consequences, the more important the action or decision is.

By this yardstick, strategic thinking and planning are perhaps the most important acts of the decision-maker. The consequences of good strategy can be the success of the organization. A poor strategy, or no strategy at all, can lead to the failure of the enterprise. As Michael Kami says, "Those who do not plan for the future cannot have one." Peter Drucker says, "The very best way to predict the future is to create it." Strategy is the key.

In every interview and study, business executives agree almost unanimously that, of all the management methods and techniques that are available today, strategic planning is still the most powerful and effective in getting business results.

Simple Tools and Techniques

One of the biggest challenges for busy executives today is finding the time to read the vast literature and master the intricacies of strategic thinking. What you need is a set of simple tools that you can use immediately to increase profitability. The twenty-one principles you are about to learn will serve as those tools.

Most companies today do not have a strategic plan, or if they do have a plan, it is outdated and obsolete in light of the current economic situation. This book will enable you to conduct a quick strategic analysis of your company and make immediate decisions to improve operations. You may even gain the insights you need to turn your company around completely, as these ideas have done for so many other businesses over the years.

TurboStrategy

Introduction

Let me begin this book with a story. In 1951, the Nobel prize-winning physicist Albert Einstein was teaching at Princeton University. He had just administered an examination to an advanced class of physics students and was on his way back to his office. His teaching assistant was walking with him, carrying the completed exam papers.

The assistant, a little shy in the presence of the greatest physicist of the twentieth century, asked him, "Dr. Einstein, wasn't that exam that you gave this class of physics students the *same* exam that you gave to this same class last year?"

Einstein thought for a moment and then said, "Yes, it was the same exam."

The teaching assistant then asked hesitantly, "But Dr. Einstein, how could you give the same exam to the same class two years in a row?"

Einstein's answer was classic. He said, "Well, the answers have changed."

The point of this story is that the questions might have been the same, but as the result of rapid developments and discoveries in world of physics at that time, the correct *answers* were different from what they might have been a year before.

Your Answers Have Changed

This story applies to you and your business as well. Your answers have changed in the last year, and they continue to change, sometimes every day. Over the course of twelve, twenty-four, or thirty-six months, your products, services, prices, processes, marketing, selling, and levels of profitability may all change. Sometimes they will all change together. This is why you need to engage in a continuous, ongoing process of strategic thinking and strategic planning.

Much of what you are doing in your business today is simply a continuation of what you have done in the past, whether or not it is the most effective and profitable way to run your business. Much of what you are doing is no longer relevant to the current business situation in today's market. The answers have changed.

Many executives are operating on old assumptions, attempting to sell their no longer ideal products and services to changed markets containing customers with different wants, needs, and expectations who are operating under new conditions with new pricing demands and constraints.

Many executives are like the driver whose companion looks at the map and says, "We're on the wrong road!"

The driver, hunched over the wheel, replies, "So what. We're making great time!"

Many executives are "making great time," working harder and harder to get results, but they're on the wrong road, going in the wrong direction in terms of the current realities. The answers have changed.

Flexibility Is Essential

The most important quality for success in business, according to the Menninger Institute, is the quality of *flexibility*. To survive and thrive in turbulent times, you must develop an attitude of open-mindedness. You must be willing to face the facts and realities of today rather than those of yesterday. You must be open to the possibility that you are on the wrong road and be prepared to change course.

According to the American Management Association, 70 percent of your decisions in business will turn out to be wrong in the fullness of time. When you made those decisions, they made sense. Based on the existing situation, they were probably good decisions. But now the answers have changed. The information upon which you based your decisions is no longer the same. The business situation may have changed dramatically.

Like calling a "time-out" in a football game, you need to stop occasionally and reevaluate the situation. You need to pull back and examine your assumptions, to determine whether or not they are still valid. With new information, you need to establish a strategic plan that is relevant and applicable to your situation today.

The One True Measure

Once upon a time, a man died of a heart attack and left his construction company to his wife. He had spent twenty-five years building the business, but he had neglected his health. He ate too much, drank too much, smoked too much, and never exercised. Finally, it all caught up with him and he was gone.

His wife had spent most of her adult life raising the children and running the home, and she knew very little about business. Nonetheless, she was now the owner of a ten-million-dollar construction company that was her sole source of support and her largest family asset.

After the funeral, she went into the company on a Monday morning, sat all the managers down and asked them to explain to her how the company worked. They realized she was serious about wanting to understand the business, so they took her around and described to her the various products and services that they offered. When they explained a particular product line that the company was selling, she asked simply, "How is it going?"

If it was selling well, she encouraged them to do more of it. If it was doing poorly, she encouraged them either to stop doing it or to change what they were doing so it was more profitable.

She had two basic questions: "What's working?" and "What's not working?"

This became her management style. Each time she came to the offices, she met with her managers or walked around and asked, "What's working?" and "What's not working?" If it wasn't working, she would instruct them to improve it or to discontinue it. If it was working, they were encouraged to do more of it.

She then began asking, "Who's working?" and "Who's not working?" In short order, she changed the staff around so that everyone was doing what they had been hired to do and making a valuable contribution. Those who would not or could not were encouraged to go elsewhere.

Practice This Method Daily

You should use the same method with your business. If, for any reason, something is no longer working, if you are not making progress, moving ahead, growing in sales and profitability, and hitting your numbers on schedule, you must ask, "Is it working?"

 If it's working, do more of it. If it's not working, be prepared to stop the clock, call a "time out" and reexamine the product, service, process, or area of activity with new eyes.

Be willing to put all of your past experiences and assumptions aside for the moment and simply ask, "What's working? and "What's not working?"

The difference between success and failure in business largely depends upon your ability to look at your company through the lens of strategic planning and make sure that everything you are doing is contributing to the achievement of your most important business goals.

Let's look now at twenty-one great ideas you can use to hold your business up to the light, perform a strategic analysis, and begin to move ahead toward your business goals of sales, growth, and profitability faster than you ever thought possible.

CHAPTER 1

Start Where You Are

Do what you can, with what you have, right where you are.

—THEODORE ROOSEVELT

The starting point of strategic planning is for you to develop absolute *clarity* about your current situation. Look at your overall business and ask, "What's working?" and "What's not working?" in every area.

What is your current level of sales? Break them down by product, product line, service, market, and distribution channel. What exactly are you selling, to which customers, at what prices, and with what level of profitability?

Compare your current sales with your assumptions, your expectations, and your projections. Are you on track? Compare your level of sales with last year. What are the trends? Are they up or down? Are they temporary or permanent? What do the trends suggest for the future of your business? What could you do to respond more effectively to them?

Cash Flow Is Everything

Look at your cash flow and levels of profitability for each product, service, and area of activity. Are your profits going up or down? Are they on budget or going sideways? Look at the percentages. Analyze your return-on-equity, return-on-investment, and return-on-sales. Are they increasing or decreasing?

Jim Collins says in *Good to Great: Why Some Companies Make the Leap—And Others Don't* that you must be willing to ask the "brutal questions" about your business if you are going to solve your problems and achieve your goals. If your goal is to build a great company, why isn't your company *already* great?

Which of your products or services is selling well today? Which of your products and services are the most profitable? Which ones are doing poorly? Which ones do you lose money on?

Is your current business situation, positive or negative, in any area, temporary, or is it part of a long-term trend? How can you know for sure? How can you find out? What should you do next?

Clarity Is the Key

Perhaps the most important word in strategic planning is "clarity." You must be absolutely clear about the answers to each of these questions. Vagueness or fuzziness in any area can lead to problems, difficulties, and even disasters.

Why has your business been successful in the past? What have you done well in the past that has been responsible for your success to date? What are the most important skills and competencies that your company possesses today? What are the very best products and services that you offer right now?

Look at the people around you. Who are your most valuable people? Who is no longer as valuable as before? Who even represents a net loss or detriment to your business? Be prepared to ask and answer the brutal questions.

The Customer Is the King

Who are your best customers today? What and where are your best markets? What do your customers like most about what you do for them? What do they compliment the most of what you offer or do for them? What is your number-one area of customer satisfaction?

What do your customers like least about what you do? What do they complain about most? What is it that you sell that your customers and potential customers prefer to buy somewhere else rather than from you?

Identify Your Personal Strengths

Look at yourself honestly. What are your own personal best skills, qualities, and abilities? What are the most important things you do at work and for your company? What are the most valuable contributions you make personally to your business?

Imagine yourself as a doctor conducting a complete medical examination on your own body. Treat your business as though it were a body as well. Get accurate information on every critical detail of your company, and use this as a baseline to determine your future actions. Be honest and objective at every step.

Harold Geneen, who built ITT into a major conglomerate, always said, "Get the facts. Get the *real* facts. Not the apparent facts, the hoped-for facts or the obvious facts. Get the real facts, based on analysis. Facts don't lie."

Question Your Assumptions

Time management expert Alex McKenzie once wrote, "Errant assumptions lie at the root of every failure." Everything you do in your business is based on certain assumptions. Some of those assumptions could be wrong. The answers may have changed, and what was correct in the past may not be correct today. Check every assumption and ask, "What if this assumption were not true?"

If you found that you were operating on the basis of a false assumption, what changes would you have to make, especially with regard to your key people, key customers, key products and services, and key projections?

Strategic planning requires that you begin with a realistic and honest assessment of exactly where you are and what you are today. This becomes your starting point for strategic planning and strategic thinking. It becomes the foundation upon which all future decisions are made.

Start Where You Are

1. What is working best in your business today? What parts of your business make you happiest?

2. What is not working in your business? What causes you the most aggravation and frustration?

3. What are your most important products and markets? What accounts for the largest portion of your revenues?

4. Who are your most important people? Who are the people who account for most of your results?

5. What are your special talents and skills? What is it you do that accounts for most of your success?

6. What are the major changes taking place in your market? What changes should you make to compensate for them?

7. What are your most treasured assumptions about your people, customers, markets, products, services, and yourself? What if one of them weren't true? What would you do then?

CHAPTER 2

Draw a Line Under the Past

Deep within man dwell those slumbering powers; powers that would astonish him, that he never dreamed of possessing; forces that would revolutionize his life if aroused and put into action.

—ORISON SWETT MARDEN

Often, when a company gets into trouble, the board or company owners bring in a *turnaround specialist* and put that person in charge. The reason they do this is because the turnaround specialist has no vested interest in anything that has happened up to that moment. The turnaround specialist simply draws a line under the past and focuses totally on the future and the survival of the business. You need to do the same. You need to be your own turnaround specialist.

To build a great tomorrow, you have to discontinue the things that aren't working. In order to do more things right, you have to stop doing things wrong.

Practice Zero-Based Thinking

For you to maintain maximum flexibility, there is a thinking tool you can use today and for the rest of your career. It is one of the best analytic tools I have ever discovered in a lifetime of reading, research, and practice. I call it "zero-based thinking."

Let me give you a quick illustration of zero-based thinking.

I live not far from a San Diego community called Rancho Santa Fe. This area has been written up in *Forbes* magazine as the most expensive neighborhood in the United States. The average home price in this area is more than a million dollars, and the prices rise quickly up to $25 and $30 million each. The neighborhood was originally established more than fifty years ago by the Santa Fe Railway Company and is considered to be the most deluxe and elite neighborhood in the greater San Diego area.

Within the *covenant* area of Rancho Santa Fe, there are very strict guidelines concerning lot size and architectural design. Each home must conform to specific rules of color and structure, and each home site must be a minimum of two acres. Since the area has been developed, and since homes have been built there for more than fifty years, there are a lot of old homes, which are often referred to by real estate agents as "scrapers."

A scraper is an older, smaller home on a lot in Rancho Santa Fe that is two acres or more in size. People who want the prestige of living in "The Ranch" have found that it is usually cheaper to simply bring in a bulldozer and *scrape* off the old house rather than attempting to fix it up or renovate it. It turns out to be cheaper to build a brand new house on the prime property than it is to try to make an old house livable.

Imagine Starting Over

Zero-based thinking requires that you apply this "scraper" mentality to every part of your business. You do this by asking this key question: *Is there anything I am doing in my business that, knowing what I know now, I wouldn't start up again today if I had it to do over?*

Instead of struggling to determine how you might modify, change, fix, revise, improve, or alter some business function, you instead ask, "If I were not doing this today, would I start it up again, *knowing what I know now?"*

To begin with, is there any product or service that you would not bring to the market, offer, or sell if you had it to do over again, starting today? Since 80 percent of your products and services are probably going to be obsolete within the next five years, there may be products and services you are offering today that, because of changed market conditions, you would not introduce if you had it to do over again, knowing what you know now. These products or services are prime candidates for discontinuation or divestiture.

Is there any *person* in your business that you would not hire, assign, appoint, go to work for, or become associated with if you had it to do over again? Most of your problems in business will come from attempting to work with or around a difficult person, who, knowing what you know now, you wouldn't get involved with again. Who does this bring to mind?

Is there any supplier, banker, or vendor you are dealing with today who, knowing what you know now, you wouldn't get involved with if you had it to do over? Since many of your business relationships will not work out over time, you must be prepared to reevaluate them constantly, especially if they are causing you any problems or frustrations.

Analyze Your Customers

Is there any *customer* you are selling to or servicing today who, knowing what you know now, you wouldn't take on again? Many companies are asking this question about their difficult customers and deciding to let them go. Sometimes one of the smartest things you can do is to "fire your customers." Encourage them to go and deal with someone else who would be more appropriate for them.

Assess Your Business Operations

Is there any *expenditure* in your business that you would not authorize again if you had it to do over? Is there any process, procedure, or activity that you wouldn't start up again, or get into, if you were making the decision today, knowing what you know now?

Is there any advertising, marketing or selling methodology, or expense that, knowing what you know now, you wouldn't start up again today? Keep asking, "What's working?" and "What's not working?"

Pay Attention to the Indicators

You can always tell when you are in a zero-based thinking situation because it causes you continuous stress, aggravation, frustration, negativity, and unhappiness. You think about it continuously. Often you bring it home at night and discuss it at the family dinner table. Sometimes it will even keep you awake at night.

Whenever something is not working, or not working out the way you expected, or causing you stress, financial losses, aggravation, or irritation, ask, "Knowing what I know now, would I get into this again today if I had it to do over?"

If the answer is "No!" then your next question is "How do I get out and how fast?"

The Decision Is Inevitable

Here's an important point. If something is not working, eventually you will have to get out of it. You will have to let the person go, discontinue the product or service, eliminate the activity or expense, or change the method of operation. It is only a matter of time. It is not going to get better all by itself. And every single executive who finally decides to get out of an unhappy situation says afterwards, "I should have done this a long time ago!"

Apply This Approach Continuously

Practice zero-based thinking as a "go forward" method for the rest of your business career. Apply it to everything you do, to every part of your business, every single day. Apply it to every product, service, process, procedure, and person, and be sure that, knowing what you know now, you *would* get into it again today if you had it to do over. If not, get out as fast as you can.

Draw a Line Under the Past

1. Imagine starting over again in every part of your business. Is there anything you are doing that, knowing what you know now, you wouldn't start up again today?

2. Is there any person in your business life who, knowing what you know now, you wouldn't hire, assign, promote, or otherwise get involved with again today?

3. Is there any product or service that, knowing what you know now, you wouldn't bring to the market again today?

4. Is there any investment you have made that, knowing what you know now, you wouldn't make again today?

5. Is there any business activity or process you are using that, knowing what you know now, you wouldn't start up again today?

6. Is there any customer or market that, knowing what you know now, you wouldn't take on or get into again today, if you had it to do over?

7. Is there any career decision you have made that, knowing what you know now, you wouldn't make the same way if you had it to do over?

CHAPTER 3

Conduct a Basic Business Analysis

Asking the right questions takes as much skill as giving the right answers.

—ROBERT HALF

Whenever you go in for a complete medical exam, the doctors and nurses follow a set procedure. They begin by checking your vital functions to determine your overall level of health. They check your pulse rate, your temperature, your blood pressure, and your respiratory rate. They then take samples and test your blood, urine, and feces. In a more extensive medical exam, they check your heart, your lungs, your colon, and a variety of other areas to get a clear picture of the health of your body. By the time they have completed their examination, they have an accurate picture of your overall health and physical well-being.

In the same way, there are basic business examination questions that you need to ask and answer continuously throughout the life of your organization. The greater the rate of turbulence in the world around you, the more important it is that you ask and answer these questions accurately.

Start with the Basics

The starting point of business analysis is for you to ask: "What business am I in?" What business am I really in? What business am I really, really in?"

Many companies become so caught up in their day-to-day operations that they lose sight of their real reasons for existence. They lose sight of the fact that they are in business to perform a particular service, or to achieve a particular goal, for a specific type of customer.

For example, many years ago the railroads concluded that they were in the railroad business. In reality, they were in the transportation business. By losing sight of the business they were really in, the railroads completely missed the shipping industry, the trucking industry, and the airline industry. It wasn't long before their markets were taken away from them by these industries, and many of them went bankrupt.

When I first began speaking, I defined myself as being in the "training" business. I soon realized I was in the "goal achievement business." My business was helping people to achieve their personal and business goals faster by providing them with practical ideas that they could use immediately to get better results.

This insight led me from talks and seminars into audio and video recording, books, training programs, and Internet-based e-learning on a variety of subjects, including the development and presentation of the Turbostrategy Process.

The Customer as Centerpiece

The next question you must ask and answer accurately is "Who is my customer?" Who is the person who buys from you today? Describe your customer in detail. What is the age, income, education, position, attitude, location, and interest of your ideal customer? Many companies are not exactly sure of the answer to this question. They have at best an unclear picture of the psychological and demographic characteristics of their customers.

Who will your customer be tomorrow if current trends continue? Who should your customer be if you want to be successful in the markets of tomorrow? Who could your customer be if you were to change, improve, or upgrade your product or service offerings?

Determine What You Sell

Your next question is "Why does my customer buy?" What value, benefit, result, or difference does your customer seek or expect to enjoy as a result of doing business with you? Of all the various benefits that your products or services offer your customers, what do your customers consider to be more important than anything else? Do you know? Your ability to define and promote this unique benefit is the real key to competitive advantage and market success.

You next question is "What do we do especially well?" What do you do better than any of your competitors? Where are you superior? Customers only buy from a particular company because they feel that, in some way, that company offers something that is superior to any other offering. What is your area of excellence?

Jack Welch of General Electric was famous for saying, "If you don't have competitive advantage, don't compete." His philosophy was that General Electric would be number one or number two in every market segment in which it competed, or the company would get out of that market. Are you number one or number two in your market? Can you be? What is your plan to achieve this market position?

Define Your Competitor

The next question, which we will deal with extensively in Chapter 10, is: "Who is my competition?"

Once you have identified your competition, you must ask why your potential customer buys from your competition rather than from you. What value or benefit does she believe she receives from someone else that she does not believe she receives from you? How could you offset this perception?

Set Clear Goals

In performing an examination of your business, you must ask, "What are my goals?" What are you trying to accomplish? If you are clear about your goals, what is holding you back from achieving them? You need clear, written, measurable, time-bounded goals for every part of your business and personal life. You need short-term, medium-term, and long-term goals. Each goal must be in writing, with plans for its accomplishment. You can't hit a target that you can't see.

Analyze everything you do in the course of a day or a week. What are the 20 percent of your activities that could account for 80 percent or more of your results? Sometimes, just 10 percent of your activities—if you were to pursue them aggressively—could account for 90 percent of your results. What might they be?

Become Action-Oriented

What actions should you take immediately in response to the answers to these questions? What is the very first thing you should do right now to increase your sales and improve your market position?

Another good question you should ask yourself is "Why am I in business at all?" Why do you exist? What social purpose does your company serve? What loss would occur to society if you ceased to do business altogether?

Imagine that you had to go in front of a government tribunal each year to justify your continued existence. What would you say to the tribunal in terms of how you serve, help, or make a difference in the lives or work of your customers to justify staying in business?

These are key questions that you need to ask and answer for your business on a regular basis. You should ask and answer these questions for yourself, as well. If you are unclear or inaccurate in your answers to any of them, the health of your enterprise could be in jeopardy.

Conduct a Basic Business Analysis

1. What are your goals for your business? What are you trying to accomplish?

2. Who is your ideal customer? Describe him or her accurately.

3. Why does your customer buy from you? What special benefits or advantages do you offer that your competitors don't have?

4. What business are you really in? Describe your business in terms of what you do for your customer and what results you get.

5. What are the 20 percent of your activities that could account for 80 percent of your results?

6. What is your competitive advantage, your "area of excellence?" In what ways are you superior to 90 percent or more of your competitors?

7. What specific, measurable actions should you take immediately in answer to the above questions?

CHAPTER 4

Decide Exactly What You Want

The world has the habit of making way for the man whose words and actions show that he knows where he is going.

—NAPOLEON HILL

Turbostrategy begins with deciding exactly what you want to accomplish in the key areas of your business life. Once you know your goals in each area, you can decide on the best steps to get there.

The GOSPA Model

You can use the GOSPA Model as a guide for strategic planning. These five key thinking tools form the basis for successful business operations.

Begin with the End in Mind

The first letter, "G," stands for **Goals**. These are the ultimate results that you want to achieve. Your goals are the end targets that you aim at

23

throughout your business year or planning period. Your goals are your sales, profits, growth rate, market share, or percentage of return on assets, equity, investment, or sales. Goals are always measurable. What are yours?

Steps on the Staircase

The second letter, "O," stands for **Objectives**. These are the subgoals, or steps, you will have to take to achieve your goals. They are like the rungs on the ladder to get to the top.

Your business objectives can be specific rates of return from advertising, levels of sales of certain products and services, number of items shipped and billed, monies collected, and cost levels for certain activities. A lower defect rate or a higher sale amount per customer can be objectives on the path to achieving the main corporate goals. What are your interim objectives?

How to Get There

The letter "S" stands for **Strategies**. These are the different approaches you can take to achieve your objectives and reach your goals. For example, achieving a specific level of profitability will require producing and selling specific quantities of products or services to a specific market in a specific way. There are many different ways to go about accomplishing these objectives. The way you choose is your strategy and may determine the success or failure of your enterprise.

Do you produce, market, sell, and deliver yourself, or do you outsource some part of the process? Do you sell direct, via retail, direct mail, catalog, or the Internet? Do you charge more, charge less, up-sell, cross-sell, or discount? Do you enter certain markets and abandon others? What is your strategy? Is it working?

Planning for Success

The letter "P" stands for **Plans**. These are your blueprints for achieving your goals. Your plans are composed of step-by-step lists of exactly what you will do, day by day, to get from wherever you are to wherever you want to go. Plans are always broken down by sequence and priority.

Some things have to be done before others can be done. Some things are more important than others in achieving the goal or objective. When your plan is organized by sequence and priority, you can accomplish much more in less time.

Business life consists almost entirely of projects, one after the other. A project can be defined as a *multitask job*, a job made up of many small jobs, each of which has to be done properly to complete the larger task. Your ability to plan, organize, and complete ever larger and more complex multitask jobs is the single most important element of your success in any field.

Develop a Bias for Action

The last letter in the GOSPA process, "A," stands for **Actions**. These are the specific tasks that you are going to complete to carry out the *plans* to implement the *strategies* to accomplish the *objectives* to achieve your *goals*.

Every important task must be clear, measurable, and time-bounded. It must be assigned to a specific person who is qualified to perform the task correctly, on time, and on budget. *What gets measured gets done.*

Focus on Profitability

The central purpose of Turbostrategy is to boost your cash flow and profits and increase your return on the money invested in your business. The aim of the strategy is to generate a higher level of cash flow and profitability than you would realize without the strategy or with your previous strategy. In short, it is to *make more money* than you are making right now from the way that you are doing business today.

The essential resources of people, money, and talent that you need to succeed in your business are always limited. They must be focused and concentrated for maximum results. This is what a good strategy enables you to do.

Four Ways to Improve Your Business

Setting strategy requires making hard decisions in four areas: First, you must decide what you are going to do *more of*. What's working? What is selling well? What products, services, and activities are the most profitable?

Second, you must decide what you are going to do *less of*. What's not working? What contributes very little to growth and profitability? What should you discontinue or eliminate based on the realities of today's market and today's customers? What can you do to reduce costs in areas where they contribute very little to results?

Third, what are you going to *start doing* that you're not doing today? What new products, services, or activities should you introduce if you want to increase your sales and profitability or improve and streamline your activities?

Finally, what are you going to *stop doing* altogether? Remember, the critical resources of time and money are always scarce. The only way you can improve results is by discontinuing certain activities altogether. You can then channel those resources into areas where they yield higher levels of business results.

Clarity is the key to strategic success. The more time you take to be absolutely clear about who you are and what you want to accomplish, the more successful and profitable you will be.

Decide Exactly What You Want

1. What are your specific, measurable long-term *goals* for sales and profitability in your business? Write them down.

2. What are the specific *objectives* of sales, staffing, production,

delivery, and customer development that you will have to achieve to accomplish your goals?

3. What are the various ways that you can meet your objectives and achieve your goals? What is the best *strategy* for you in today's market?

4. What should you do *more of* and really focus on to increase your sales and profitability?

5. What should you do *less of*, based on your current experience? What's not working?

6. What should you *start doing* that you are not doing today? What opportunities are available to you?

7. What should you discontinue, and *stop doing altogether*, so that you can free up resources for more profitable activities?

- Continue
- Keep
- Stop
- Start

CHAPTER 5

Design Your Ideal Future

We have been endowed with the capacity and the power to create desirable pictures within and to find them automatically printed in the outer world of our environment.

—JOHN McDONALD

Some time ago, I conducted a strategic planning session for the senior executives of a $172 billion company. The organization was going through a period of considerable turbulence caused by change, competition, and new government regulation. There had been layoffs, firings, downsizing, and divestments. My clients were the top executives who had survived the recent turmoil, and the bloodletting was not yet over. In these circumstances, they were both worried about the future and distracted in the present.

Create a Five-Year Fantasy

To get them centered and focused, I began the strategy session with a process that I call "idealization." In this process, which you can use yourself, I had the members of the top team create a "five-year fantasy."

"Let's put aside the current situation for the moment," I suggested. "Instead, tell me what this company would look like five years from now if it were perfect in every respect?"

This exercise forced them to take their attention away from the problems of the present and focus their thinking on the possibilities of the future.

As we went around the room, each person contributed an idea about what the company would look like if it were perfect. I wrote each idea on a flip chart and taped the pages onto the walls where everyone could see them. In less than half an hour, we generated twenty-seven ideal descriptions.

We then voted on these idealized goals and organized them by priority. We ended up with a series of clear objectives, including *highly profitable, tremendous market reputation, high stock price, top leadership, fabulous customer service, great place to work, best management, rapid growth rate, and top reputation in the industry,* among others.

Think in Terms of Possibilities

I then asked them, "Are these goals possible?" One by one, they agreed that all of these goals were possible in five years. They might not be achievable in one or two years, but in five years, every one of them could be accomplished with will and determination.

We came out of that session with everyone revitalized and committed to working on achieving one or more of those five-year *fantasies.* Over the next two years, the company completely reorganized. They did more of some things and less of others. They started doing things that they had not done in the past, and they stopped certain activities altogether. They took complete control of their corporate destiny and changed it.

Think About the Future

Future-orientation is a key element of strategic planning and strategic thinking. It is a major responsibility of leadership and top people in every area. Only the leader can think about the future. Only the leader can plan for the future. There is no one else in the organization who can do it, and if the leader does not think about and plan for the future as an ongoing part of his job, it will not be done. As they say in Alaska, "Only the lead sled dog ever gets a different view."

How often and how well the top people in the company think about the future are the factors that largely determine the success or failure of the business. If you don't know where you're going, any road will take you there.

The development of the quality of future-orientation requires that you create an ideal image of your company sometime in the future. You project forward three to five years in your mind and imagine that your company is perfect in every respect. You decide exactly how much you would be selling and earning at that time. You imagine your ideal stock price, your ideal reputation in the market, your ideal work situation, and your ideal human environment.

Back-from-the-Future Thinking

Once you have a clear picture of your ideal future, you return mentally to your current situation and think about what you would have to do, starting today, to turn your future vision into a current reality. This is called "back-from-the-future thinking."

Make a list of all the things that would have to happen for you to realize your fantasy sometime in the future. It is amazing how your perspective changes when you look back from the future, exactly as if you were looking back from the top of the mountain at yourself down in the valley and seeing the exact route you would have to follow to get to the top.

Leaders Have Vision

In 3,300 studies of leaders reviewed by James MacPherson, searching for the common denominators of leadership throughout the ages, the one quality that all the leaders had in common was **vision**. Leaders have vision; non-leaders do not.

Becoming a visionary requires that you develop the ability to imagine, define, articulate, share, and inspire other people with an exciting picture of the future. You get everyone in your business committed to fulfilling this vision and to working toward it every day. This is the key to leadership and to building a great company.

Aristotle wrote, "We become what we repeatedly do." You become a leader by thinking the way leaders think, both in your business and in your personal life. You become a leader by thinking about the future and about how you can make it a present reality.

Create an Exciting Picture

The Bible says, "Where there is no vision, the people perish." This doesn't mean that they lie down and die. It just means that they lose heart. They lose their commitment and enthusiasm for giving of their best. When their managers do not clarify and articulate an exciting vision for the company, people just go through the motions at work, doing only what they need to do to keep their jobs.

Unfortunately, many companies have no vision at all. They may have started with an exciting vision of accomplishing something that had never been done before, but over time, buffeted by the waves of a turbulent market, they have lost sight of their reason for existence, which is to make a meaningful difference in the lives and work of their customers.

Instead of continuously defining and articulating the company's vision, the key decision-makers become focused on day-to-day operations. They think only about survival. They even say that they don't have time for "the vision thing." They are too busy fighting fires.

Now, More Than Ever

But it is in times of rapid change, and turbulence in the market, that an exciting vision of the future becomes more important that ever before. A vision can become the force that binds people together into a solid team. It can give meaning and purpose to work, even when times are tough and pay increases are not possible.

There are many ways you can approach the development of a vision for your organization. Perhaps the very best vision for your company includes two key components. First, it is focused on your customers and on doing something for them that changes and improves their lives or work in some way. Second, it contains a commitment to *excellence*, to being the very best at doing whatever you do for your customers. These are the keys to vision.

Your vision is to "be the best!" at the most important thing you do for your customers. Your vision is to serve your customers in such a way that you are seen as superior in a particular product, service, or activity. Imagine that you could be known as *outstanding* in any one thing that you do for your customers. What would it be? Your answer can be the starting point of a vision for your business that changes your future completely.

Your Personal Vision

You need a vision for yourself as well. Project forward five years in your imagination. If your future were perfect in every way, what would it look like? If your income, your position in your company or field, your family life, your health, your job, and every part of your life were ideal in every way, how would it be different from today?

Once you are clear about your vision, for yourself and for your business, the only question you ask is, "How do I make it a reality?" Top people think continuously in terms of *how?* They think in terms of taking action, of *what* can be done.

Once you have clarified your vision and determined what you will have to do to make it a reality, you then do something every day to move you toward the creation of your ideal future. You take complete control of your destiny. As Drucker wrote, "The very best way to predict the future is to create it." And the starting point is vision.

Design Your Ideal Future

1. What is your vision for your company? Project forward and imagine that your business were ideal in every way. What would it look like?

2. What is your vision for yourself? If your life and career were ideal in every way, what would they look like?

3. Idealize in each area of your business. If your products, services, sales, and profitability were perfect, what would they look like?

4. Idealize with regard to your people. If your staff were ideal in terms of skills, abilities, personalities, and results, how would they be different from what they are today?

5. Imagine that a major magazine were going to write a story about your company. What would you want them to say?

6. Project forward five years and then look back to today from that vantage point. What would you have to change today to create your ideal future?

7. In what one area would it be most helpful to sales and profitability if your company were widely known as "the best"? What steps could you take immediately to begin earning that reputation?

CHAPTER 6

Create a Mission Statement

If one advances confidently in the direction of his dreams, and endeavors to live the life which he has imagined, he will meet with a success unexpected in common hours."

—HENRY DAVID THOREAU

Viktor Frankl, a survivor of Auschwitz and the founder of Logotherapy, concluded after a lifetime of research and experience that the deepest need of each person is for *meaning and purpose* in life. This is equally true for an organization made up of different people with different backgrounds.

A mission statement is essential for your company because it gives the people in the company this sense of meaning and purpose. A mission statement gives guidance and direction. It inspires loyalty and commitment. It tells people what you are and what you stand for. It gives a reason and a focus for corporate activities and daily work.

Your Declaration of Purpose

Your mission statement is an expression of the company's aspirations and the purposes for which the company exists. It is a present-tense declaration of what the company wants to become and what it wants to accomplish sometime in the future. It is an ideal expression of your reasons for being in business in the first place.

Your mission statement emerges from the vision and values of your business and then describes the future in tangible terms. A good mission statement contains a *measure* of some kind so that you can tell whether or not it has been achieved and what progress you are making.

Determine Your Values

You begin the development of a mission statement by determining your values. A value is an organizing principle around which you build your life and make your decisions. Your values lie at the very core of your being and define you as a person. Over time, your outer world becomes a reflection of the person you really are inside. As the Old Testament says, "As he thinketh in his heart, so is he."

One of the major differences between people who succeed greatly in business and average, or below average, people in business is that top people are very clear about their values. They know *who* they are and *what* they stand for. They also know what they will *not* stand for. They have a strong sense of right or wrong. They are confident and uncompromising when it comes to making decisions based on their values.

What are your values? What are the three to five values that your company believes in and stands for? In my strategic planning work with many corporations, the same values seem to emerge over and over. The most commonly held values in business are *integrity, quality, excellence, customer service, caring about people, profitability, innovativeness, and high self-esteem.*

A Business and Its Beliefs

In his book about IBM, *A Business and Its Beliefs*, Thomas J. Watson, Jr. gives the three founding values of IBM as "Excellence, Quality Service, and Respect for People." These three values have been the guiding principles of IBM since its first day in business. You could make almost any mistake in your career at IBM as long as you did not violate one of the values. Everyone who worked at IBM took pride in living and practicing these values at work and with their customers. They were instrumental in making IBM a great company.

Once you are clear about your values, you define what each of them means in terms of actions and behaviors. For example, if your value is *integrity*, you could define integrity as follows: *We treat everyone inside and outside the company in an honest and straightforward way, and we always strive to develop and maintain a reputation for fair dealing with employees, customers, suppliers, bankers, and government agencies.*

Thereafter, whenever you have to make a decision in which the value of integrity is a key factor, you revisit your value statement and follow its guidelines. A client of mine once said something quite profound, which I never forgot, "Integrity is not really a value in and of itself. It is rather the value that guarantees all the other values."

Build on a Solid Foundation

Once you are clear about your values—and you don't really need more than three to five values to start—you craft a mission statement based on them. This statement expresses what you want to become and accomplish and how you will behave in the fulfillment of your mission.

Here is an example of a mission statement: *We are a high-integrity company, devoted to our people and our customers, and our mission is to be the national leader in sales and profitability of high-quality security systems for the American household and family.*

Every mission statement must have a *measure* of some kind against which you can gauge your progress. If your goal is to "be the national leader," you must determine how much you will have to sell each month and each year in order to be number one in your industry.

When both Lexus and Infiniti entered the U.S. car market, their individual missions were to become number one in the JD Power Customer Satisfaction Survey. Within three years of entering the market, Lexus and Infiniti *tied* for the first place in the JD Power awards. They achieved their goals and fulfilled their missions.

Involve Other People

The more people you can involve in crafting and editing the mission statement, the greater commitment and loyalty they will have to living by it, day by day. Hold meetings where employees contribute their ideas and opinions about company values. Discuss and vote on these values, selecting the ones most popular and important to everyone. Craft your company mission statement to be consistent with the key values that your employees believe in.

Once your mission statement is developed, you can put it everywhere as a statement to people, both inside and outside the company, of your vision, values, meaning, and purpose. You can publish it in your promotional materials and put it on your Web site. You can hold it up as an object of pride.

The Fortunate 500

When Ken Blanchard and Norman Vincent Peale got together to create what they called "The Fortunate 500," they studied companies from many different industries. They discovered that the companies in each industry which had *written* statements of their values, and mission statements that everyone in the company knew, were consistently more profitable than those companies that did not have values at all, or did not have them in writing.

Companies with clear values and written mission statements seem to operate more efficiently, treat each other and their customers better, achieve greater customer loyalty, find it easier to borrow money, and generally do better in good times and bad.

Create Your Personal Mission Statement

As an individual, you should have a personal and family mission statement as well. You should have a clear idea of what you believe in and stand for and what you are dedicated to accomplishing with your life and for your family. This should be in writing and should be regularly revised and updated as your family life and situation change. It can make a wonderful difference in your life.

Create a Mission Statement

1. Determine your personal reasons for doing what you do. What gives you a sense of *meaning and purpose* in life?

2. Decide upon the three to five key values upon which your company is based. Involve other people in the discussion.

3. Define the actions and behaviors that people will engage in, both inside and outside the company, that are consistent with your values.

4. Design a mission statement, an ideal description of what your company wants to accomplish for its customers sometime in the future.

5. Write out a list of your values, and what they mean, plus your mission statement, and share them with your staff and customers.

6. Create a personal mission statement for your career. What do you want to accomplish, and how do you want to be known?

7. Create a mission statement for yourself and your family. What is it that you want to accomplish or achieve with your family in the years ahead?

CHAPTER 7

Reinvent Your Organization

Every man of genius sees the world at a different angle than his fellows . . ."

—HAVELOCK ELLIS

Jack Welch of General Electric once said, "If the rate of change *outside* your organization is greater than the rate of change *inside* your organization, then the end is in sight."

In times of turbulence, you should be prepared to reinvent your business as often as necessary as your external world changes. As an exercise, imagine that you were starting your business over again today. What would you get into? What would you not get into?

Bundle of Resources

For greater perspective, stand back and view your business as a *bundle of resources* and capabilities, like a fire hose of talent and ability that can

41

be aimed in many directions to achieve different results. Instead of limiting yourself to seeing your business as an organization that is designed to perform specific functions, producing and selling certain products and services, think of it as being capable of doing a variety of things that are completely different from what you are doing today.

The Great Fire

As you think about reinventing your business, imagine that your company burned to the ground while you were away. When you arrive at the scene, you find that all your staff are safe and standing in the parking lot.

As it happens, there is unoccupied office space available across the street. You can immediately move into the new space and start your business anew. Here is the question: Which of your products and services would you begin producing and distributing right away, and which ones would you not start up again, knowing what you know now?

Examine Every Relationship

If you were starting your business over again today, completely free from any encumbrances of the past, which customers would you call first, and which ones would you not call at all? Which vendors, suppliers, bankers, or other people would you immediately get in touch with, and whom would you call later, if at all? What would you do first? What would you do second? What would you *not* start up again, knowing what you know now?

Reinvent Your Staff Relationships

Now, let's go back to the parking lot. Let us assume that all of your people are safe and standing around waiting for instructions. Which of them would you take across the street with you to the new business, and which ones would you leave in the parking lot? Who would be the first and most important person whose services you would want to secure? Who would be the second most important? Who would be third? And so on.

Examine Your Organization

If you could reinvent your business, what would you do *more* of? What would you do *less* of? What would you *start* doing that you are not doing today? What would you *stop* doing altogether?

In reinventing your organization, ask yourself, "What are my most important talents, skills, abilities, and core competencies, and *what else* could I do with them? Who are my best people and what else could they do?"

Keep thinking about how you would reinvent your business if you were starting over. This will keep you on the cutting edge of creativity and innovation.

Think in Terms of Excellence

The key questions in reinvention are, What could you be absolutely excellent at doing in today's market? Where could you be the best? Where could you achieve world-class quality? Where could you be better than 90 percent of your competitors?

The market only pays extraordinary rewards for extraordinary products and services. Where and how could you do what you do in an extraordinary fashion?

Reinvent Your Career

Finally, think about reinventing yourself and your career on a regular basis as well. If you were starting over again today, what would you do more of or less of? What would you start or stop? What would you get into? What would you get out of?

If you were starting your career over again, what additional knowledge and skills would you want to have? What can you do, starting today, to acquire those key skills? Imagine that you could do a variety of jobs. What would you *really* like to do with your life?

Since you are going to have to reinvent yourself regularly throughout your career, it is very important that you think about how you would do it well in advance of when it becomes necessary.

Reinvent Your Organization

1. If you were starting your business over again today, what would you do differently?

2. If you were starting your career over again today, what would you get into or out of?

3. If your business burned to the ground and you could offer only *one* of your products or services, which one would it be?

4. Who are your most important customers, the ones you would immediately move to take care of, if you were starting over?

5. Who are your most important people, both inside and outside of your business?

6. What are your most important contacts and business relationships, the ones you would most want to preserve if you were starting over?

7. If money were no object, what steps would you take today to reinvent your business?

CHAPTER 8

Select the Right People

Here lies a man who knows how to enlist into his service people better than himself.

—ANDREW CARNEGIE'S EPITAPH

The people in your company are the most important parts of your business. All work, all performance, all results come from them, both as individuals and when they work together in teams of some kind. The manager's output is the output of his or her team and of the individual team members.

In business, people come first. Jobs, activities, and results are only achieved after the right people are in place. Jim Collins says in *Good to Great* that the key to building a great business is "first, get the right people on the bus, and second, get the wrong people off the bus." Any other approach is bound to fail.

Two Key Qualities to Look For

The best people have two qualities. First, they can be counted on to get the job done, to get it done well, and to get it done in a timely fashion. Second, they get along well with others. They are good team players.

You should apply zero-based thinking to each person who reports to you on a regular basis. Continually ask, "Knowing what I now know, would I hire, assign, or promote this person again, if I had it to do over?"

If the answer is "No," your next question is, How do I remove or replace this person, and how fast can I do it?"

Hire Slowly

In picking the right people to be a part of your team, select them carefully. Take your time. Harvey McKay, in his book *Swim With the Sharks Without Being Eaten Alive,* tells about interviewing thirty-five people for a sales position and then deciding to hire *none* of them because he had not yet found the ideal candidate. Sometimes the best people decisions are the ones you don't make in the first place.

In politics, they say, "People are policy." This is true in private business as well. The people you select are an expression of your personal values and philosophy. Your people choices tell everyone around you what kind of company you have and what kind of management you are building for the future. Take your time.

Thoughtfulness is a key quality of excellent executives. This is especially true when picking people to fill important slots. You can dramatically increase the quality of your hiring decisions by taking ample time up front to think through the job.

Think Through the Job

Begin by defining the job in terms of the exact outputs and results required. Think of the job as a pipeline, with time, money, and resources going in one end, and specific results coming out the other end. What do you want and need those results to be?

Once you are clear about the results you desire, set specific measures of performance on each job and each task. How will you and the candidate know whether or not the job has been done properly? Remember: What gets measured, gets done. And: If you can't measure it, you can't manage it.

Examine Past Performance

Once you are clear about the results you expect and the standards of performance you will use to measure success in the fulfillment of the job's responsibilities, you can determine the exact skills and abilities the candidate will have to have to get those results. And, as Peter Drucker says, "The only true predictor of future performance is past performance."

When applying for a job, most people judge themselves in terms of what they think they can do in the future. But this is not a luxury you can afford. You must be disciplined in focusing on what the person has already done successfully. This should be your primary consideration in making any hiring decision.

The Law of Three

There is a powerful principle you can use to increase your likelihood of making better hiring decisions. This method slows down the process and improves the quality of your ultimate choices. It is simple, powerful, and incredibly effective. I call it the "Law of Three."

First, before you decide to hire a person, interview the candidate at least three times. The first time you interview a person, she will look and sound the very best she will ever be. Since we are all primarily emotional, we are often overly influenced by an attractive candidate, even to the point of impulsively making a hiring decision. Keep reminding yourself that fast hiring decisions are usually wrong hiring decisions.

Second, and in conjunction with the above, once you decide that you like a particular candidate, interview the person in three different places. A candidate who shines in your office during the first interview may begin to fade during the second interview down the hall in a meeting room or across the street over a cup of coffee.

Hire in Haste, Repent at Leisure

Earlier in my career, the president of a large company tentatively offered me a position of considerable responsibility. But before he met with me to discuss salary and my job description, he suggested that I take a drive with him to his working farm outside the city. We ended up spending about three hours driving out there and walking around the farm, chatting casually the whole time. At the end of this "interview," he offered me the job. This was his way of taking enough time to "get a feel" for how he and I would get along later.

A Stroll in the Park

Some years later, I was negotiating to conduct a strategic planning session with the president of a billion-dollar company. All the key executives of the company would be brought together for three days at a distant resort. The future of the company would be discussed in depth.

Suddenly, he stood up and said, "Let's go for a drive."

He told his secretary to have the car pick us up in front of the building. He then instructed the driver to drop us outside the city park. We got out and went for a walk lasting almost an hour, chatting about family and philosophy, looking at the flowers, just strolling around. At the end of the walk, he said, "Okay. It's a deal. Let's make the arrangements."

We drove back to the office, finalized the agreement, and everything worked out well. Again, this was his way of doing a "gut check" on me and the work I could do for his organization.

Never Decide Alone

Once you have met with the preferred candidate three times and have met with him or her in three different places, the next part of the Law of Three is for you to have *three* other people interview the person. Never rely solely on your own judgment. Always invite the opinions of others, especially others who will be working with the candidate if you should hire him.

Sometimes, a person who looks good to you will reveal aspects of his personality to potential coworkers that he covers up with you. In many cases, I have had my staff reject a person who I thought was ideal for the job. I have never overridden a "thumbs down" from my staff, and I've never regretted it. They have saved me from myself many times.

Check References Carefully

Finally, after three interviews, in three places, and with three different people, check at least three references before you make a final decision. If the previous employer will not give you any information for fear of legal problems, there is one question you can always ask: "Would you hire this person back again?"

If the answer is not an unequivocal "Yes!" proceed with caution. Ask the candidate why the previous employer would not hire him back. Listen carefully to the answer. It may be decisive.

Go for the Gold

When seeking a person for an important position, look for an "outperformer." Look for someone you like and who you feel can do the job really well. Refuse to settle for anyone less than what you consider to be the ideal person. Only hire someone who fits in, and someone around whom you can build your department or your business.

Look for team players, people who work well with others. Look for the demonstrated ability to perform and execute, to get the job done without supervision or day-to-day hands-on management.

Clarity and Consideration

Once you hire a person, start her off strong. Tell her exactly what you want done and how you will measure it. Work with her personally, or assign someone else to work with her until she gets her feet on the ground. The bad old days of "sink or swim" are gone forever. Human assets are too precious to squander.

The primary reason for low motivation and poor performance, assuming that the individual has the ability to do the job, is lack of clarity regarding the results expected. The primary reason for high motivation and excellent performance is absolute clarity with regard to the results expected.

In turbulent times, with rapid and discontinuous change all around you, you should continually revisit the job description and the results expected of each person. Never assume that everyone still knows exactly what it is that you want or need.

There is a direct relationship between motivation and commitment on the one hand, and the opportunity to discuss the job on the other. The more you involve people in discussions about their work, the more motivated they will be, and the better they will do the job.

Select the Right People

1. Rank everyone in your company on a scale from one to ten, with ten being the highest, on their competence at their job.

2. Resolve to build a team of highly motivated, competent, and positive employees to help you get the results you need.

3. Think through each new job or hire carefully in advance. Write out the description clearly.

4. Interview at least three candidates for a new position. Interview the candidate you like at least three times, in three different places, and have him or her interviewed by at least three other people.

5. Check references carefully. Seek the fatal flaw or weakness that could make the candidate unsuitable.

6. Hire only positive, likable people; they make the best team players.

7. Results are everything. Continually emphasize and explain exactly what results are expected from each person.

CHAPTER 9

Market More Effectively

Because its purpose is to create a customer, the business enterprise has two—and only these two—basic functions: marketing and innovation. Marketing and innovation produce results; all the rest are costs.

—PETER DRUCKER

All business strategy is ultimately marketing strategy. Whenever you are worried about the health or future of your business, get back to thinking about marketing and selling. Focus single-mindedly on increasing sales and revenues. Cutting expenses and controlling costs is an ongoing necessity, but you can't cost-cut your way to business success. You have to increase cash flow, and this only comes from selling more of your products or services.

No matter how challenging or competitive the economy appears, as much as 80 percent of your market is still untapped. There are almost always hidden opportunities around you. The ability to uncover and take advantage of those opportunities is the true test of the competence of an executive or a business.

Four Keys to Marketing

There are four essential elements of marketing. These are: *specialization, differentiation, segmentation, and concentration.* You must implement and execute effectively in all four areas to survive and thrive in your business. A lack or weakness in any one area can lead to underachievement and even the failure of the enterprise.

Decide Who You Are and What You Do

Specialization requires that you focus on specific products or services, specific markets, or specific customer needs. You must fight the temptation to try to offer too many products and services to too many customers in too many areas. You must specialize, both in your own mind, and in the mind of your customer.

What is it *exactly* that your product or service is designed to achieve, avoid, or preserve for your customer? What are the core competencies or proprietary methods or technologies that enable you to specialize in this area? What specific problem or need can you solve or satisfy for your customer? And of all the different results you can get with your business, where do you—should you—could you—specialize?

Many companies work very hard to master an area of specialization that is highly valued by a particular type of customer. It may take several years of hard, dedicated commitment to build a successful business around this core competency. But then some companies develop the "walk on water" mentality and begin thinking that they can produce other products or services equally well. In no time, a company can begin to diffuse its energies and resources, moving out of the area of specialization where it is successful into areas it neither knows nor understands.

Determine How You Can Be Superior

You *differentiate* your product or service by determining exactly how you are going to be superior to your competitors. I'll explain this process in detail in Chapter 11. It is the key to business success and high profitability.

Choose Your Best Market Segment

The process of *segmentation* requires that you clearly define the exact customers who can *most* benefit from what it is that you do better than anyone else. This requires rigorous customer analysis to determine who your best potential customers are today and who they can be tomorrow.

Focus Your Resources

Concentration requires that you focus your vital resources of time, talent, and money on marketing and selling more and more to your very best potential customers. Sales efforts directed to your highest probability prospects yield the highest possible return on your activities. Based on your decisions on specialization, differentiation, and segmentation, where should you concentrate your marketing and selling efforts?

Reevaluate Constantly

All marketing strategies eventually become obsolete and stop working. If your sales are down for any reason, it may be time for you to revisit your answers in one or more of these four areas. This can lead to your developing a more effective marketing and selling strategy, one that works in today's market.

Remember, today *the answers have changed* with regard to your market. Changes in customer demand, competition, or other market forces may require that you change your area of specialization, your area of differentiation, your ideal customer segments, and your areas of focus and concentration. You may have to change more than one of these at the same time.

See Yourself as a Business

In your personal life, you should ask the same questions of yourself as well. What is your personal area of *specialization*? In what way is your work *superior* to that of your competitors? What is the *ideal* position or area of responsibility for you to apply your talents? Where should you be *concentrating* your energies to get the very best results and the greatest rewards possible?

Especially, you should continually ask yourself, "What is it that I do very, very well?" What is your personal area of excellence? What could it be? What should it be?

Looking Ahead

Looking into the future of your business or industry, what new competencies do you need to develop to lead your field in the months and years ahead? What additional knowledge and skills do you need to acquire? What are those few tasks which, if you did them in an excellent fashion, would have the greatest positive impact on your career? In what areas could you be paid the most for the application of your special talents and abilities? This question is just as relevant for you as it is for your company.

Market More Effectively

1. Decide today to *dominate* your field, to be the best at marketing and innovation in your product or service area. What is the first step you should take?

2. Determine your area of specialization, by product or service, market, or type of customer. What should it be? What could it be?

3. How do you differentiate your product or service from those of your competitors? In what ways are you superior to anyone else? What could your area of superiority be? What should it be?

4. What are you best market segments? Where are your highest probability customers? Who can benefit the most from using what you sell?

5. How can you organize your business so that you concentrate your marketing and selling efforts on those customers who can buy and pay faster than any others?

6. What additional products, services, knowledge, or capabilities will you need to dominate your markets in the months and years ahead?

7. What should you immediately start doing more of or less of, and what should you start or stop doing to adjust to the current market?

CHAPTER 10

Analyze Your Competition

Concentrate your strengths against your competitor's relative weaknesses.

—BRUCE HENDERSON

There is a military adage that "No strategy ever survives first contact with the enemy." No business strategy ever survives first contact with the marketplace either. It must always be adjusted to deal with the realities of the moment.

You have probably heard it said that "business is war." What this means is that there is vigorous and never-ending competition to conquer the market, win the customer, and achieve the sale. Just as you are eager to succeed by selling your product or service and earning a profit, so is your competitor. She wants your business—if possible, *all of it*. To achieve this, your competitor will do or offer almost anything to take your customers away from you.

59

Know Your Enemy

Here then is a question for you: Who is your competition? Exactly? Your choice of competitor determines almost everything you do in your market, just as the choice of an adversary determines everything a general does in the process of conducting military operations.

Your competitor determines what you offer and where you offer it. Your competitor determines your prices and how you charge. Your competitor determines your levels of profitability and how consistently you earn them. Your competitor determines your rate of growth and your very survival. Everything you do must be done with a view toward your existing or potential competitor and his or her likely responses to your actions.

Determine Customers' Buying Motives

Once you have determined why it is that people buy from *you*, you must then answer the question "Why do people buy from my competitors?" What value or benefits are your potential customers convinced they receive when buying from your competitor rather than from you?

What are your competitor's key strengths? What are his areas of specialization, differentiation, segmentation, and concentration? What does your competitor have that you don't have? What does he offer that you don't offer? What is he doing more of or better than you? What is his unique selling proposition?

Marketing Myopia

Many people dismiss or ignore their major competitors. They criticize or belittle them when their names come up. Often they think and say that customers who prefer competitive offerings are simply ignorant or misled. As a result of this self-inflicted myopia, they fail to observe and learn how to outdo their competitors in tough markets.

One of the most effective business strategies you can implement is to always *admire* your successful competitors. Never dismiss them out of hand. Study them. Learn from them. Respect what they are doing well, and look for ways to improve upon their best features.

Offset Competitors' Advantages

As you study your competitors, look for ways to offset or neutralize the advantages their customers perceive them to have. What are your competitors' weaknesses? How can you exploit these weaknesses? What do you do better than they do? In what ways are your products or services superior to their offerings? In what areas do you have a distinct advantage over your competitors? What can you do to offset your competitors' strengths and maximize your own advantages? How can you better position yourself against your competitors in a tough market?

The more time you take to study and understand why and how your competitors are successful in selling to your customers, the more likely it is that you will find an opportunity to take away their market share. As Sun Tzu says in *The Art of War*, "If you know both yourself and your enemy, you will prevail in a hundred battles."

You Must Be Clear

The greater clarity you develop with regard to your competitors' strengths and weaknesses and to the reasons your potential customers buy from them, the better able you will be to counter them and compete effectively. Rigorous competitive analysis can be a vital key to business success. In its absence, you will always be at a disadvantage.

Analyze Your Competition

1. Who is your competition with the exact customers you are trying to attract?

2. What would happen if you changed your offerings in such a way that you targeted a different group of customers who would be easier to sell to?

3. Why do your potential customers buy from your competitors? What advantages do they perceive?

4. What are your competitors' unique selling propositions? What special feature or benefit do their products or services have that yours does not?

5. In what ways are you superior to your competitors? What can you offer that they cannot? How can you emphasize this advantage in your sales and marketing efforts?

6. Where are your competitors vulnerable? How could you exploit their vulnerability to your advantage?

7. How could you alter your marketing strategy in such a way that you could achieve dominance with a specific customer or market segment in a particular area?

CHAPTER 11

Do It Better, Faster, Cheaper

The man who comes up with a means for doing or producing almost anything better, faster or more economically has his future and his fortune at his fingertips.

—J. PAUL GETTY

The most important single determinant of success is your area of *competitive advantage*. It is more important than all other factors. It determines the rise or fall of your business, your level of profitability, your position in the marketplace, and everything else you accomplish.

Your competitive advantage must be crystal clear to you and to everyone in your company, as well as to your prospective customers. Lack of clear competitive advantage leads quickly to diminished sales, loss of market share, lower profitability, price-cutting, and, ultimately, business failure.

Your High Concept

Your business was started because you or your company had an idea for a product or service that was different from or better than other products and services. Your company offered to satisfy the same need or to solve the same problem better, faster, or more cheaply than anyone or anything else then available.

Your ability to differentiate your product in the minds and hearts of your customers is the key to winning them in the first place and keeping them after the initial sale. To buy from you, a customer must be convinced that, all things considered, your offering is different from and better than anything else that is currently available at the same price. Jack Welch was famous for saying, "If you don't have competitive advantage, don't compete!"

Price as a Differentiator

Low price does not give you a competitive advantage all by itself. A product that sells solely on the basis of price is called a *commodity*. In the eyes of the customer, it is identical to any other product or service offered by any other company. The only way that a commodity can be differentiated is on the basis of price. Whenever a product becomes com-moditized in the marketplace, it becomes almost impossible to charge enough for it to make a worthwhile profit.

Fortunately, what you sell is *special*. It is not a commodity. It is different in many ways from anything else available, if only because the people who make and sell it are different.

However, whenever the key people in a company, or the salespeople for that company, are unclear about why and how their product or service is different from and better than competitive products, they resort to price-cutting to get the business. There is no future in that direction.

Your Central Focus

The critical role of marketing is to differentiate your product or service from those of your competitors. Any marketing, advertising, or selling that does not emphasize the valuable differences contained in your product as compared with that of your competitors is a waste of time and money.

All differentiation revolves around the creation of a clear, competitive advantage of some kind. This is the central focus of all strategic thinking with regard to marketing.

Three Areas of Differentiation

To succeed in a tough market, what you sell must be superior to your competitors' offerings in at least *three* ways. It must be better, faster, cheaper, and easier to use in some way that makes it more attractive than rival products or services. It must be sold more professionally or serviced with greater sensitivity, speed, or efficiency. It must be better in at least three areas.

One of your key jobs in strategic thinking is to identify the three areas in which you are better and then to emphasize those areas of superiority in all of your marketing and sales work.

Three Potential Areas of Superiority

In *The Discipline of Market Leaders* Michael Treacy and Fred Wiersma identified three areas where market leaders are superior to their competitors. They concluded that each business, to achieve market dominance, must be excellent in at least one of these areas and reasonably good in the other two.

Achieve Operational Excellence

The first discipline they identified is *operational excellence*. A company with this competitive advantage is able to run its business so efficiently and well that it can produce and sell its products and services at lower prices than its competitors. The company can then pass on the cost savings to its customers in the form of lower prices or keep the savings in the form of higher profits—or both.

Companies like McDonald's and Wal-Mart, for example, are operationally excellent. Each has been able to achieve such economies of scale via mass production (McDonald's) or superior distribution systems (Wal-Mart) that they dominate their markets.

How could you achieve operational excellence in your business, or some part of your business, in such a way that you could be the low-cost provider in your market? How could you dramatically reduce your costs of doing business and use this low-cost advantage to increase your sales and profitability?

Lead the Field

The second area where you could achieve competitive advantage is in the use of *innovative technology* leading to the production of high-quality products and services. Companies like Mercedes and Rolex fall into this category, as do Sony and Lexus.

Customers are willing to pay a premium for a brand name that represents high quality and cutting-edge technology. Where are there opportunities for you to distinguish your products or services by using your imagination to become the quality leader in your field?

Be Close to the Customer

The third area where you could develop competitive advantage is in being "close to the customer." This requires that you invest the time to develop high-quality relationships based on "customer intimacy." Customers will pay more and remain loyal longer to companies that seem to know and understand them better than others. Providers of specialized services, such as consulting firms, law firms, and accounting firms fall into this category.

In what ways could you develop higher levels of trust and credibility with your customers? What could you do to demonstrate to your customers that you really care about them and their interests? This strategy can offer a breakthrough opportunity, especially in the sale of expensive products and services where resales and referrals are possible.

Pick Your Targets

To lead your field and achieve higher levels of profitability, you have to be outstanding in one of these three areas and very good in the other two. One of the most important decisions you make is to choose your area of competitive advantage and then dedicate your company to achieving it.

A competitive advantage has two qualities. First, it is something you offer that your competitors do not offer to the same degree. It is clear that you have an advantage in that area. Domino's Pizza developed a competitive advantage based on speed of home delivery that no competitor was able to match. With that advantage, Domino's went on to build 7,000 outlets, making its founder, Tom Monahan, a billionaire in the process.

Second, a competitive advantage is something that customers recognize, appreciate, and are willing to pay a premium to enjoy. In every case, it is the customer who decides if your competitive advantage is important to him or her. The customer will tell you if your offering is superior to that of your competitors in some way by buying your products or services in sufficient quantity to enable you to profit and grow.

Define Your Terms

A product or service that is "better" is a product that does what the customer purchases it to do in a way that is superior to the product of any competitor. Apply this to your company. In the view of your customers, are your products and services "better" than anything else that is available to them?

The quality of being "faster" means that your product or service satisfies the "need for speed." It achieves the result or benefit promised by your product faster than your competitor does. It is sold, serviced, or delivered faster. Domino's Pizza built its success around its reputation for speedy delivery.

If your product is "cheaper," it means that you offer the same value at a lower cost. You may offer better terms, or even greater value, at the same cost. Perhaps you offer superior service included in the same price that your competitors charge. Perhaps you offer additional benefits that make your product or service appear cheaper than that of your competitor. As a result, your customer feels that he or she would be better off buying from you rather than from someone else.

If your product is "easier," this means that your customer can acquire or use it with greater convenience. The customer gets the results and benefits you offer with less effort. Perhaps the customer experience is smoother and more enjoyable as well. In buying from you, there are "no hassles." The customer perceives this as a value that is worth paying for.

Strive for Superiority

Your area of excellence is the key to your success in a competitive marketplace. This is where your product or service stands out in comparison to that of your competitors. It is a value or benefit that you offer that no one else offers. With regard to your products or services, what is your area of excellence? What could it be? What should it be?

Your area of superiority is defined as an area of performance where your product or service is superior to that of your competitors. This performance difference is significant enough that your customer will buy it and even pay you more for it. In what way does your product perform better, in terms of getting results that your customer cares about, than that of your competitors? How could you improve the performance of your products or services in some meaningful way?

You can be excellent without being superior. You can be superior—as in the areas of speed or cost—without being excellent.

Finally, your unique selling proposition is something that you and only you offer to your customers, and it is something that they really care about. No one else does as well as you do in this area. No one else achieves the same benefit or result. What is your unique selling proposition? What could it be?

The Keys to Success

Every product or service, in order to survive in a competitive market, must have an area of excellence, an area of superiority, and a unique selling proposition. The development and maintenance of these competitive advantages is the primary job of management.

You should always be prepared to answer the customer's primary question: "Give me one reason why I should buy from you rather than from someone else."

Whatever your answer is to that question, you should build all your marketing and sales efforts around it. Your answer is the key to business success.

Look into Yourself

On a personal level, you must continually ask these questions of yourself. What is your personal area of excellence? Where are you superior to your competitors? What is your unique selling proposition? In what ways do you do your job better or faster than others? What is it that you *and only you* do in an outstanding fashion for your company? What could it be? What should it be?

Perhaps the most important area of superiority you can develop is your ability to do your job quickly and well, in an excellent fashion, consistently and dependably every time. This is the key to success as an individual in a competitive marketplace.

Do It Better, Faster, Cheaper

1. In what ways are your most important products or services superior to those of your competitors?

2. What is your recognized "area of excellence?" If you were to conduct a survey, what would people say that your company does especially well?

3. In what ways are your products or services faster to acquire, use, and enjoy than your competitors'?

4. What is your unique selling proposition? What is it that your products or services offer that no other company can match?

5. In what ways are your products or services cheaper to buy and use? In what ways do they achieve superior financial results for your customers for the same cost?

6. If you were known for being outstanding in any one area of your product or service offerings, what one distinction would have the greatest positive impact on your sales and profitability?

7. List the three areas where your products are—or can be— superior to those of any of your competitors. What is your plan to achieve this area of market superiority? What should you do first?

CHAPTER 12

Change Your Marketing Mix

Marketing . . . is the whole business seen from the point of view of the final result, that is, from the customer's point of view. Concern and responsibility for marketing must therefore permeate all areas of the enterprise.

—PETER DRUCKER

There are four critical elements that determine how much you sell, how much you charge, how much profit you make, how fast you grow, and the entire future of your business. Each of these elements must be constantly revisited in response to competitive pressures in your fast-changing markets. They are in a continuous state of flux. They seldom remain the same for any period of time. The answers are always changing.

These elements are called the *marketing mix*. They are the factors that determine the success or failure of your marketing efforts. You must be constantly thinking about changing one or more of them as markets and competitors change. They all start with the letter "P."

What Do You Sell?

The first part of the marketing mix is your **product** or service. Always define your product or service in terms of what it "does" for your customers, versus what it "is." Here's the question: "Is your product or service, as you are offering it today, ideally suited for your current market and customers?"

Remember, if it works, it is already obsolete. If your product or service is popular and profitable, it is already being replaced by your competitors. Because of the dynamics of the market, they will be aggressively seeking ways to offer something to your customers that is better, faster, or cheaper than your successful products. Your competitors are staying up at night thinking about how to take your customers, grab your markets, and put you out of business. As Tarzan said to Jane, "It's a jungle out there!"

Be Fast on Your Feet

Because of this competitive pressure, within five years, approximately 80 percent of all products and services will be new or different from what they are today. Many businesses that are thriving today will be memories five or ten years from now because their products will become obsolete and unwanted in a fast-moving market. Companies will fail to replace their products fast enough and will be left in the dust of those businesses that move more quickly.

A serious problem with many companies is that they fall in love with their product and with their history. They "get married" to the process of producing and distributing their products and services. They dismiss challenges to their products, thinking that customer loyalty is strong enough to withstand superior competitive offerings. As a result, they fail to respond fast enough to their competitors when they come out with something that customers prefer. Don't let this happen to you.

The Market Test

There is a simple way for you to know if your product or service offers what customers want in today's marketplace: It is selling well! There is a steady and growing demand for what you sell. People want it. The orders keep pouring in. It is relatively easy for your salespeople to sell, and your level of customer satisfaction is high.

If these conditions do not exist, you have to reexamine your product and service offerings. Always be open to the possibility that the market is passing you by and that you need to develop new products and services quickly if you want to survive and thrive.

How Much Do You Charge?

The second part of the marketing mix is your **price**. Is your price the right price for what you are selling? Should you change your price in some way? Should you increase it, decrease it, combine your price with other items, or add items to your price? Should you change your terms or offer something different for the same price?

Be open to the possibility that the way you have priced your products or services in the past may not work any more. You may have to sell your products or services with more generous down payments and extended payment terms. You may need to accept trade-ins on a different basis. But you must do whatever it takes.

Whenever you see a sale or a price reduction of any kind, it is an admission by the company that they guessed wrong about the price that customers were willing to pay. They are now guessing again by lowering the price, hoping that this is the price at which they can sell everything they have available. If they do not clear their inventory at the new price, they will guess again by lowering the price once more.

Double Your Price?

One of my clients was offering a magazine for an annual subscription of twenty-four dollars and losing money with every issue, hoping eventually to make a profit by selling more advertising. The business advisor studied the market for this type of specialty publication and then suggested that they double the price. This was an avenue they had never considered.

After a good deal of soul-searching, they took a deep breath and doubled the price of the annual subscription. Because the magazine was so well liked by its subscribers, less than 10 percent of them canceled. Overnight, they went from losses to profits and changed the entire future of the company. Is there any place in your business where you could increase your prices and still hold onto your market?

How Do You Sell It?

The third element of the marketing mix is **promotion**. This word embraces everything you do in the process of marketing, advertising, and selling your product or service. You may have a superb product at a great price, but you can go broke quickly if your method of sale is wrong or inadequate.

The key to business success is for you to have a good product or service and then vigorously, aggressively, and continuously offer it, promote it, and sell it in every reasonable way possible. This is usually the make-or-break area of business activity.

How are you currently promoting and selling your product or service? What's working? What's not working? Should you change your methods of advertising, marketing, selling, or acquiring customers in any way?

Sell More Stuff

Especially, should you upgrade and improve your direct-selling methods, people, presentation, and capabilities? Very often, a rapid improvement in your selling methodology is the key to turning your business around.

You have heard it said that "Nothing happens until a sale takes place." Stripped of all business theory, the key to business success is to "sell more stuff." One of the keys to the success of the Turbostrategy approach is to organize and reorganize your business and activities so that there is a total focus on selling and generating revenues. Cash flow is the lifeblood of the business, and cash flow comes from sales.

Train Your Salespeople

The sad fact is that approximately 70 percent of salespeople in America have had no sales training at all except for product training. About 95 percent of them could dramatically improve their sales if they were better trained in certain elements of the sales process. This explains why the most profitable companies invest the most in sales training, and the least profitable companies don't. When you send a poorly trained or untrained salesperson up against a professional, the untrained person doesn't have a chance.

Is Your Phone Ringing?

In addition to little or no sales training, many companies either do too little advertising or their advertising is not effective. It does not attract qualified customers in sufficient quantity. Sometimes a change in the advertising message, or in the medium being used, can increase responses by several hundred percent for the same amount spent.

Some years ago, partners of mine were spending a lot of money on a poorly designed radio campaign that had been sold to them by the station. The offering was vague and unclear. The wording was poor, and the narration was not convincing. One day they received a call from an advertising expert who asked them how the campaign was going. With the usual bravado of entrepreneurs, they assured him that it was a great success. He then said, "I have only one question for you: 'Is your phone ringing?'"

As it happened, the phone was silent. No one was responding to the advertising. They were losing money they could not afford to lose.

Within one week, following the advice of this specialist, they rewrote and re-recorded the advertising spots. From then on, the phone fell off the hook. It saved their business.

Ever after, when I think about the effectiveness of advertising, I always ask, "Is your phone ringing?" No matter what anyone says, this is still the best measure of how effectively your advertising is working for your company.

You can have the finest product in the world, but if you are not vigorously and aggressively promoting and selling it, it will sit on the shelf and gather dust. On the other hand, you can have an average product, but if you are selling it well, you can have a thriving business.

Where Do You Sell?

The fourth element of the marketing mix is the **place**. This is the specific location where the sale of your product takes place. Where exactly do you sell your product today? Do you sell in homes, offices, or in your own retail establishment? Do you sell in a particular city or state or nationwide? Do you sell in stores or by direct selling or by direct mail? Most important, should you change the place at which you offer your products?

IBM and Apple used to sell exclusively through their own sales forces. Then they changed and began offering their products through retail computer stores. Meanwhile, the only way you can buy a Dell computer is by phoning the company or contacting them via the Internet. They then send the equipment to you. In each case, the selection of the correct location from which to sell the product was a core part of their marketing strategy.

Perhaps you need to change or improve the place at which you are selling your product or service. Sometimes you need to sell it somewhere completely different from where you are selling it today. A change in the location at which you offer your product or service could change the direction of your business. What could it be?

Examine Your Assumptions

Whenever you have difficulties selling a sufficient quantity of your product or service, you should examine all of your assumptions in the areas of product, price, promotion, and place. You should be willing to consider the possibility that your method is completely wrong in one or more of these areas.

It often happens that a single change in one of the "P's" in the marketing mix can change the entire nature of your business, boost your results, increase your profitability, and move you toward market leadership. Keep an open mind.

The Answers Are Changing

What is the correct marketing mix that will enable you to sell the very most at the highest cost and earn the greatest profit? The answers are changing with incredible speed, every year, and even every month. Each action of the competitors in your market changes the dynamics of what you must do now to survive and thrive.

With every major or minor shift in your market, all bets are off. Scott McNeely of Sun Microsystems said recently, "In an entrepreneurial business, every assumption has to be revised or thrown out every three weeks." What assumptions are you going on that may no longer be true?

Change Your Marketing Mix

1. Be prepared to challenge every aspect of your marketing, especially if it is not working as well as before. What areas cause you the greatest frustration and dissatisfaction?

2. What exactly do you sell, defined as what it "does" for your customers, versus what it "is"?

3. What prices do you charge? How could you change the way you charge to make buying from you more attractive?

4. How do you promote your product? Could there be better ways of advertising your products or services that would give you better results?

5. How do you sell your product or service? Is every person who deals with your customers fully trained in every key result area of selling?

6. Where do you sell your product or service? Should you be exploring other locations or methods of sale?

7. Should you change more than one of the elements of the marketing mix at the same time? Challenging market conditions often call for bold departures from the methods of the past, especially if they are no longer working.

CHAPTER 13

Position Your Company for Success

Man is not the creature of circumstances. Circumstances are the creatures of men.

—BENJAMIN DISRAELI

In their book *Positioning,* Al Ries and Jack Trout explain that the way you are positioned in the hearts and minds of your customers and potential customers determines your success or failure in competitive markets more than any other single factor.

Dr. Theodore Levitt, dean of the Harvard Business School, wrote in *The Marketing Imagination* that your most valuable asset is "how you are known to your customers, your reputation in the market." Your reputation is a value that people will pay for.

Whenever you read about a company with $1 million worth of assets selling for $10 million, you are witnessing an example of how valuable

79

a reputation can be. The extra $9 million is officially called "good will." That extra payment for good will means that the name of the company is so valuable that the purchaser is willing to pay a significant premium for the company because of its reputation in the marketplace.

What Others Say

It is estimated that 84 percent of purchase decisions today are based on *word of mouth*, or how other people talk about your products and services among themselves. The whole purpose of advertising is to get people to try your products or services initially with the hope that they will be so satisfied that they will buy again and will also tell others.

Dr. Robert Cialdini, in his book *Influence: How and Why People Agree to Things,* explains that "social proof" is a major influencing factor determining whether or not people buy or do not buy a product or service. The most important part of social proof is the perceived similarity of the person recommending the product to the person hearing the recommendation. For example, if you are an executive and you learn that "other executives" rate a product or service highly, you will be more influenced to try it than if you heard that "doctors" or "lawyers" had used it and approved of it.

Successful companies give a lot of thought to the way they want customers to think and talk about them. They organize all of their marketing and selling activities around generating and creating a perception in the mind of the prospect that leads to purchases and repurchases.

What Words Do You Own?

Professor Leon Festinger of Harvard developed a concept that he called "attribution theory" to explain how people make decisions and come to conclusions. He found that people usually think in terms of a phrase or even a single word when they think of a particular product or service. Whatever this word happens to be has an inordinate impact on their decision to buy or not to buy.

For example, IBM means "excellence." McDonald's means "convenience." Nordstrom's means "service." Federal Express owns the word "dependability" in overnight delivery. Deliberately or accidentally, each product or service develops a reputation that positions it against its competitors. What is yours? You "own" a word when customers immediately think of your company or product when they hear that word.

Choose Your Words Carefully

Reis and Trout suggest that you select the word or words that you want to *own* in the mind of your market and then do everything possible to seize and take control of those words, defending them against all comers.

For example, my teenage sons have a single criterion for movies. It is the word "action." If it is an action picture, they will see it. If it is not, they are not interested. My older daughter prefers movies that are designated as "romance" movies or what she sometimes calls "chick flicks." My youngest daughter, who is ten years old, only wants to go to "children's" movies. If you want to attract them, you have to position your movie with those words.

Mercedes owns the words "quality engineering." BMW owns the words "ultimate driving machine." Domino's Pizza owns the words "fast delivery." In every case, these companies have built their success on creating and maintaining this perception in the minds of their customer markets.

Create Your Own Cheat Sheet

Here is the question: What words do *you* own? What words *should* you own in the hearts and minds of your prospective customers? What words *could* you own if you were to reorganize and redirect your marketing efforts?

As an exercise, imagine one of your prospects meeting with one of your customers. Imagine that your customer called you and asked what you would like her to say to your prospect to convince him to buy from you?

If you could put together a "cheat sheet" with the exact words or phrases you would like your customer to leave in the mind of your prospect, what words would you choose? Would you choose words like *excellent quality, high integrity, friendly service, nice people, quick responses to problems, easy to work with, great prices?* How do you want to be described by your customers and potential customers? Of all the words and phrases that customers could use to describe your products and services and your company, which would be the most helpful for you and your business?

Once you are absolutely clear about the positioning that you want to achieve, you must organize every customer interaction, every product and service, every element of sales, delivery, and distribution so that those words are the final impression left in your customer's mind. This is the key to positioning yourself for great success in a competitive marketplace.

What Is Your Brand?

A brand represents a value and is based on trust between the company and the customer. When the customer buys a "brand name," she is confident that she will get exactly what the company promises. Your brand summarizes how a customer thinks and feels about you. It cannot be built overnight, as the dot-coms tried to do with Super Bowl advertising. By throwing huge sums of money at a 50-million-person audience, the dot-coms tried to build quickly the kind of long-term reputation enjoyed by established companies. But building a brand (trust) requires a series of personal experiences with you and what you sell. A brand takes years to develop in the hearts and minds of your customers.

This value and trust are the result of the customer's experience with you and your products over time. It is very much like a personal reputation in that it takes a long time to build. It can be damaged or even destroyed by a negative experience.

Creating Your Brand

There are two parts to the branding experience. First, there are the *promises* you make when you induce your customer to buy from you for the first time. These are the claims and value offerings contained in your advertising and selling activities.

The second, and more important, part of branding consists of the promises you *keep* when you deliver your product or service. Philip Crosby, author of *Quality Is Free*, says that quality means that "Your product does what you say it will do when you sell it, and it continues to do it." This is the essence of branding.

Creatures of Habit

There is a rule that says that *people decide emotionally and then justify logically*. In this sense, customers are lazy. Once they are perfectly happy and satisfied with a product or service offering, they will go on buying that product or service indefinitely. In their minds, it is too much effort or trouble to change.

The most successful companies are those that have established a brand that people can depend on absolutely. Whether it is a local restaurant or a multinational corporation, customers feel comfortable buying from them as the result of happy buying experiences in the past.

Everything Counts

Your positioning against your competition, your reputation, and your branding determine how much you sell and how easy it is for you to sell that amount. They determine how much you can charge and how fast you grow. A company with a superb reputation can charge more because people place a dollar value on a good brand. Think of French perfume, Japanese or German cameras, Swiss watches, or Tiffany jewelry.

Here's the rule: Everything counts! Everything you do in your interactions with your customer helps or hurts. Everything adds up or takes away. Everything either improves your positioning and the customer perception of your products or services and of your company, or it detracts from them. Nothing is neutral. Everything counts. You must therefore leave nothing to chance.

The Brand Called "You"

These principles are very much the same in your own life and career. Your personal positioning in the minds of the key people in your business life largely determines your level of success, your rate of pay, your speed of promotion, and almost everything that happens to you in your career.

How are you described and thought about by others when you are not there? What is your *personal brand?* What is your reputation? How do other people think and speak about you, both as a person and as a contributor to the organization?

In your work, the best branding or reputation you can have is that people know that you can be absolutely depended upon to do an excellent job every single time. Personal performance is the key. You do what you say you will do, and you keep on doing it, like the Energizer Bunny.

Larry Bossidy says in *Execution: The Discipline of Getting Things Done* that the most valuable quality or characteristic of an executive is his or her ability to take action and get results, to execute the plan exactly as expected. This is the key to your personal branding as well.

Position Your Company for Success

1. What is your company's reputation in your market? How do customers and competitors think and talk about you?

2. What words do people use when describing your products or services to others?

3. If you could "own" certain words that apply to your company and your products or services, which words would you choose?

4. What words, if they were automatically associated with your company, would have the greatest positive effect on your sales and profitability?

5. What changes would you have to make to ensure that every customer contact reinforced the message that you wanted to send to your customers about doing business with you?

6. What are the most important promises that you make to your prospects to get them to buy from you for the first time? Do you keep these promises after the sale?

7. What are the most positive things that your customers say about dealing with your company? How could you create a system to ensure that more customers say these things?

CHAPTER 14

Develop Strategic Business Units

There is no security on this earth; there is only opportunity.

—GENERAL DOUGLAS MacARTHUR

The strategic business unit (SBU) concept has revolutionized many multiproduct or multiservice businesses. It is a way of thinking that is absolutely vital to business success. It was first developed by the Boston Consulting Group and then used by many Fortune 1000 companies to transform their organizations into more efficient and vastly more profitable companies.

With the SBU concept, each product or service is made into a separate business unit within the company. These business units are then grouped with similar products or services in one of three ways: 1) by common characteristics or features; 2) by common markets; or 3) by common customers to whom the products or services are sold.

Businesses Within the Business

Each unit is then managed as a separate business, with its own management structure, strategic plan, business goals, sales and revenue targets, levels of profitability, and key roles and responsibilities of the people within the unit.

The starting point of implementing the SBU method is to make someone specifically responsible for the operations and the results of the unit. A competent person is put completely in charge of attaining a certain level of profitability, exactly as if he or she were being made president of a separate business.

Basic Business Planning

To make the SBU approach work, you begin by drawing up a complete business plan for each unit. Each product or service within the unit must also have a complete business plan that includes estimated sales revenues, costs, and profitability. You then proceed to determine the exact people and resources that will be necessary to achieve the goals of this SBU.

Make Someone Responsible

The primary reason that a product or service succeeds is that a competent person is completely responsible for it and is totally committed to its success. A major reason for the failure of any product or service is that the responsibility for its success or failure is spread among several people, and no one is accountable. No one person has a meaningful stake in the outcome.

To be assured of realizing the full potential of a product, service, business unit, or any new venture, you should always begin by putting someone in charge whose rewards are tied to the success of the project.

Reevaluate Your Entire Business

When you first introduce the SBU concept, you have an opportunity to stand back and reevaluate your entire company by placing each of your products and services in one of four categories.

These categories are defined using two grids. First, a product can have *high* growth potential—the products of tomorrow—or *low* growth potential—the products of yesterday.

Second, the products can be defined as being *users* of cash or *suppliers* of cash. With this classification methodology, you now have four categories of products and services. These are delineated by the Boston Consulting Group as *cash cows, stars, question marks, and dogs.*

The Cash Cow

The first type, *the cash cow*, is defined as an established product or service that sells well and is a net contributor of cash to the business. It is not growing in sales and profitability nor is it declining. It is a mainstay of the company. It is a key to the company's success. At one time it may have been the main product or service of the company, but now it is simply a dependable source of revenue.

Your strategy with your cash cows is to devote sufficient resources and people to them so that their ability to contribute sales and cash to your business extends as long as possible. Many companies make the mistake of taking their cash cows for granted and end up losing sales and revenues that would have been easy to maintain.

Reach for the Stars

The second type of product or service, a *star*, is also a net contributor of cash. It differs from a cash cow in that it has tremendous potential for growth and profitability. It is the kind of product that, properly positioned and promoted, can be a major source of revenue and cash flow in the years ahead.

Examine your complete range of products and services, especially the newer ones, and ask, "Which of these has the potential to be a big seller?" What would you have to do or invest in to help make it a major source of sales and revenues?

Neither Success Nor Failure

The third type of product is the *question mark*. This is a product or service that is a user of cash. Although it is not yet profitable, it has great potential if it can be properly developed, marketed, and promoted.

Question marks are products that have not yet become successful. They can fail, taking all the investment put into them for research, development, and market testing down the drain. One of the most important goals you achieve with the SBU concept is to identify your question marks and decide whether to get in deeper or to get out altogether.

Here is an important point. Most new products, services, or business ventures either fail completely or, at best, fail to realize the expectations companies had for them when they were conceived. Many new ideas turn out to be successful in ways completely different from what was initially envisioned when the decision was made to invest in them.

In fast-growing markets, when there are high levels of business activity and positive cash flows, you can afford to carry products or services that are question marks. But when the market tightens up, you must become both cautious and cold-blooded about any business activity that is not carrying its weight. You must be prepared to "fish or cut bait." You must be willing to cut your losses quickly to assure the survival of the enterprise. This is no time for self-delusion. Hope is not a strategy in tough competitive markets.

Dogs Drag You Down

The fourth category of strategic business unit is the "dog." This is a product or service that loses money and has no future in the marketplace of today or tomorrow. It seemed like a good idea at the time it was introduced. Sometimes a good deal of emotional investment and capital has been put into this product or service, but it is clear to almost everyone that it has no future.

The dogs should be eliminated as quickly as possible. The people and resources currently being spent on them should be focused on the products and services that have a greater probability of generating cash and profitability in the future.

When a turnaround specialist takes over a troubled company, he gets rid of the dogs immediately. This often frees up enough cash and people to return the company to solvency in a few weeks or months. You should do this as a regular part of management.

Take Immediate Action

The SBU concept is simple. First, take excellent care of the cash cows. Don't take them for granted. Do everything possible to assure that they remain healthy for years to come. Invest in them if necessary to upgrade them and maintain their attractiveness to their core customers.

Second, do everything possible to promote the stars. Put your best talents and energies behind helping the stars to realize their full potential in the market. Assign one of your best people and make him or her responsible for each star's success. Be sure to provide whatever resources are necessary to sell as many of your stars as possible before your competitors move into this market.

Third, resolve the question marks as quickly as possible. It is always necessary to invest in research and development for the products of the future. But there comes a time when you have to make a decision to proceed or to stop trying. Establish clear criteria for decision-making about new and existing products and stick to them.

The fourth SBU concept has to do with the dogs. Once you have decided that a product or service has no future, you should discontinue it immediately. You can then channel the people and resources working on it into areas where greater success is possible. Keep asking yourself, "If I had not already committed time and money to this product, knowing what I know now, would I start investing in it again today?"

Implementing the Process

The SBU approach to your business requires that you first group your products and services into separate business categories, based on similarities they have in common. You then evaluate every product or service on its own merits, determining whether or not it is a cash cow, a star, a question mark, or a dog.

You insist that each product, and each grouping of products, stand on its own as a separate, profitable business unit. This SBU approach enables you to see each part of your business clearly and to make better decisions. You use the concept of profitability as your primary measure.

One of the major reasons that companies get into trouble is that they bunch too many products together in a single basket where it becomes almost impossible to determine where the profits stop and the losses begin. The SBU concept will help you to avoid this danger.

See Yourself as Multitalented

Apply the SBU concept to yourself and your career. You have several areas of talent and ability, core competencies, experience, knowledge, and education. What are your "cash cows," the skills that are central to your value to the organization?

What are your "stars," the emerging areas of activity or new skills and knowledge that can make you extremely valuable in the future?

What are your potential areas of great success? What are the projects, responsibilities, and areas of opportunity that, if you exploit them fully, can enable you to move ahead more rapidly in your career?

Finally, what are the "dog" areas of your work life? These are the tasks or skills that you may have mastered in the past but that distract you from your future. These are the jobs and activities that take up a lot of time but that are nowhere near as valuable as other things you could be doing. What are they?

Develop Strategic Business Units

1. Begin today to view each product or service as a separate business, responsible for generating a certain amount of profit every month.

2. Group your different products or services by similar characteristics, similar customers, or similar markets.

3. What are the cash cows of your business? What are the core products or services that are essential to your overall profitability?

4. What can you do today to safeguard and nurture your cash cows to assure that they continue contributing sales and cash flow far into the future?

5. What are the stars of your business? What are the products that are selling well, increasing in market share, and generating high profits?

6. What could you do to increase the sales and profitability of your stars?

7. What are the question marks of your business? Which of your current products or services should you discontinue, knowing what you know now?

8. What are your dogs? What products or services should you discontinue altogether?

CHAPTER 15

Sell More Effectively

Presenting a professional, upbeat face to the public does wonders for the way people perceive your business.

—STEVE ESTRIDGE

Sometimes I ask my management audiences, "If you were selling twice as much as you are today, could you fill all the orders?" In most cases, the business leaders will all agree that they could quite comfortably deliver twice as much of their products or services with their current resources than they are currently selling.

I then ask them, "Well then, why aren't you selling twice as much? What is holding you back?" They often just look at me blankly, as if that were something that had never occurred to them.

Your Untapped Market Potential

The fact is that probably 80 percent of your potential customers have not yet been approached by your sales or promotional efforts. Most of them don't know about you and don't know how much better off they could be with your product or service. No one has told them.

You could probably be selling twice as much as you are today if you could just figure out how to do it. This is your main job.

The Great Sales Question

When I conduct marketing strategy with my clients, I give them this key sales question to answer. It has taken me twenty-five years of study and experience to devise this question, and it deals with every part of the sales and marketing process, like a formula or recipe. By answering this question, you can conduct a quick analysis of your sales situation—past, present, and future. Here is the question:

> "**What** is to be sold **to whom** and **by whom**, and **how**, and **at what price** and how is it going to be **paid for** and **delivered** satisfactorily?"

The failure to answer any one part of this question accurately can lead to a complete failure of the sales effort. Unfortunately, most companies cannot answer the whole question correctly.

What Is to Be Sold?

The first part of the question is **"What is to be sold?"** To answer this correctly, you have to define your product or service in terms of what it *does* and how it benefits your customer. How does it improve his or her life or work? Of all the benefits that a customer enjoys from purchasing your product or service, what is the primary benefit, the one thing that you offer that makes you superior to any other competitor in the marketplace? Do you know the answer to this?

Who Is Going to Sell It?

The second part of the question is **"By whom?"** Who is actually going to sell the product or service and get the check from the customer? How are you going to recruit, train, manage, field, and support the salesperson? How is this salesperson going to uncover the necessary leads and get face-to-face with the prospective customer?

The salesperson is like the foot soldier in the army: Before you go to war, you have to think carefully about how this soldier is going to be recruited and supported, and exactly what the salesperson is going to say and do when she gets face-to-face with someone who can buy what you are selling.

Who Is Your Customer?

The next part of the question is "**To whom?**" Answering this requires that you define your *ideal* customer clearly and focus your sales efforts on this specific type of person. You should have a clear psychographic and demographic profile of the person who is the most likely to buy your product or service, the prospect who can benefit from it most readily. Without this clarity, your salespeople will be like machine gunners, spraying the market, calling on many people who are not prospects at all.

How Much Are You Going to Charge?

The next part of the question is **"At what price?"** Sometimes the answer to this question is fixed and cannot be changed. In many cases, however, the way you price your products and services is a key factor that determines your level of sales and profitability.

As the market changes, or in response to either customer reaction or competitive pressure, you must be prepared to revisit your prices as often as necessary. Imagine that you were starting over again today to set your prices, knowing what you now know about the current market. Is there any price you would raise, lower, or modify in some way?

Collecting Payment

The next part of the question is **"How is it going to be paid for?"** Do you require payment in full in advance? Do you require a deposit when the sale is made with the balance to be paid at a later time on certain terms? Do you offer credit or financing? Especially, what do your competitors do?

Often a change in the way you charge, or in your pricing structure, can dramatically increase your sales. What could you do differently in today's market that would make it easier or more attractive to buy your product or service?

Delivering the Goods

The final part of the question is **"How is going to be delivered satisfactorily?"** What is the exact process of getting the product or service to your customer in such a way, and at such a level of quality, that the customer both buys from you again and recommends you to others?

An improvement in customer satisfaction at the point of delivery and afterwards can greatly increase your sales in the future.

Undoubtedly, you think constantly about these questions and how you might answer them more effectively. The health of your business is largely determined by how appropriate your answers are today in the face of a changing market.

Building a World-Class Sales Force

The linchpin of this entire process is the sales effort. Unfortunately, many companies are run by people who have never been salespeople themselves. For this reason, they have no understanding of the central importance of the sales effort. They think that you just place a couple of ads, hire a couple of salespeople, and the business just rolls in the door. They are often baffled when sales fall off, no one responds to the advertising, and the salespeople don't sell anything.

All successful, profitable companies, without exception, have superb salespeople. These people have been carefully recruited by top professional managers. They have been thoroughly trained, sometimes for many months. They are professionally managed, day-by-day and week-by-week, by excellent sales executives who know exactly what they are doing, based on many years of experience. Sometimes, just bringing in a new sales executive or manager can boost sales dramatically and transform the results of an entire company.

Your ability to field a world-class sales team is the key to your success in any market. This is an area that requires real focus and attention, never more so than when the market becomes tougher and more competitive.

The Pivotal Skill

Building an effective sales force, from the initial recruiting through the training and on to the day-to-day management, is both an art and a science. It is the pivotal skill in any company that depends on sales for the success of the business. The sales force is like the engine of the automobile. Its horsepower and efficiency determine the speed and effectiveness of the entire vehicle.

Many companies transform their results by focusing single-mindedly on the sales effort. They set clear parameters for the kind of salespeople they want, recruit carefully, train them thoroughly, and manage them professionally. As a result, their sales and cash flow increase dramatically, and they can weather any market.

Sell More Effectively

1. What is the exact process necessary to sell your product or service, from the first customer contact through to the close of the sale? Do you know? How could it be improved?

2. What must your prospective customer be convinced of before he chooses your product over that of your competitor?

3. If money were no object, what special results or benefits could you offer in your sales efforts that would make your product more desirable than any other available?

4. What is your process for recruiting salespeople? What media do you use? What levels of education and experience do you require?

5. What kind of compensation system do you have for salespeople? What is it based on? How could it be improved so that it motivates better sales performance?

6. How much of your business comes from referrals from happy customers? How could you increase the number of referrals you get as a percentage of your business?

7. Why aren't your sales twice as high already? What sales efforts could you make to tap into that 80 percent of the market that has never heard of you?

CHAPTER 16

Eliminate the Bottlenecks

Success in solving the problem depends on choosing the right aspect, on attacking the fortress from its accessible side.

—GEORGE POLYA

In physical terms, a single blockage of a key artery can lead to a heart attack and the death of an otherwise healthy individual. Some years ago, James Fixx, a leading authority on jogging for physical fitness, one of the top runners in America, in Olympic condition, dropped dead of a heart attack while running at the age of fifty-two because of a single piece of plaque that came loose and lodged in his heart.

In every respect, James Fixx was one of the healthiest and fittest human beings on the planet. But one blockage was sufficient to end his life. This same principle applies to businesses, careers, and one's personal life as well. One fatal flaw can cost you a lot, if not everything.

Identify Your Limiting Factor

In your business, for example, there are almost always critical constraints or "limiting factors" that determine how fast you achieve your goals. Not only can a constraint slow you down and keep you from achieving the sales and profitability that you desire, but a serious constraint can bring your business to its knees.

Identifying what is holding you back, and removing it, can help you to achieve your goals faster than almost anything else you can do. Once you learn the art of *constraint analysis*, you can use it for the rest of your career.

Follow the Formula

You apply the process of constraint analysis to your business by following certain steps. First, you decide on your specific business goals. Make them clear, measurable, and time-bounded.

Second, you ask yourself, "Why am I not at that goal already?" What is holding you back? What is the constraint, chokepoint, or bottleneck that determines how fast you achieve the specific goals of sales, cash flow, or profitability in your business?

Let us return to my earlier question: Would you like to double your sales and double your income? If your answer is "yes," then why haven't you done it already? Why aren't your sales twice as high? Why aren't your profits twice as high? What is holding you back? What is constraining you? What is the limiting factor?

Bottlenecks Exist Everywhere

In every complex activity, from the production process of a huge factory to the job of getting from home to work in the morning, there is a limiting factor or constraint of some kind that affects the *speed* at which you achieve your goal. This bottleneck or chokepoint determines how fast you get the result you desire, and it often determines the success or failure of the entire process.

The elimination of a single constraint can speed up the rate at which you get the results you desire so vastly that it will amaze both you and everyone around you. One of the most important strategic thinking exercises you engage in is constraint analysis, learning to identify and focus on the one activity that can help you achieve the desired result faster than ever before.

Internal vs. External Constraints

The 80/20 Rule applies to constraints. Approximately 80 percent of the constraints or limiting factors in your company's ability to achieve its goals are *internal*, not external. Approximately 80 percent of the reasons why you are not doubling your sales and doubling your profitability are *inside* your organization. Only about 20 percent are outside in the external marketplace or are caused by external factors.

These internal constraints may be contained in the work process itself. Perhaps it needs to be revised partially or completely so that it functions faster and more efficiently. The constraint to business growth could be the lack of a particular person or skill. Sometimes the addition of one highly competent person in a particular area can transform the results of the whole business.

Incompetence as a Constraint

The reverse might also be true. The constraint might be the presence in a key job of an incompetent person no one has the courage to confront or remove. It is amazing how many businesses get into serious trouble, or even go broke, because of the unwillingness to deal effectively with an incompetent person.

Your constraints may be a lack of sales or marketing ability. You may have a good product or service, but you don't have skilled people to sell it. Many companies go out of business for this reason alone.

The Wrong Product

Your internal constraint could be a product or service that is inappropriate for today's market. No matter how hard you work or how competent your people are, there are simply not enough customers for what you are trying to sell. The answer to alleviating this constraint on sales and cash flow is to develop or offer something for which there is greater demand among your potential customers.

Your constraint could be inefficiencies in production and delivery that lead to rising costs or reduced revenues. It could be defects in your products or services that are causing customer dissatisfaction, product returns and refunds, problems with payment, and other difficulties.

Take Charge of Your Situation

Only 20 percent of your problems and constraints are *outside* of your business and your direct control. Only 20 percent of your problems are caused by the marketplace, your competitors, or other external factors. This is not to say that important external factors may be limiting your growth and profitability, but the place to start looking for your problems is *within* your organization, before you begin looking outside.

It is absolutely essential for business success that you identify and focus on your major constraint or chokepoint, whatever it may be at the time. Bring all of your energy and attention to bear on alleviating the one factor that is setting the speed at which you achieve your most important business goals. Success in this area can give you a greater payoff than anything else you can do with the same time and energy.

Constraint analysis and removal can make the difference between business success and failure. It is a key part of the Turbostrategy process. One of the worst things you can do is to identify and focus your attention on the *wrong* constraint, leaving the *real* constraint in place.

Identify Your Personal Constraints

Think about your personal life and goals as well. Ask yourself, "What are my most important goals? Why am I not there already? What is it *within me* that is holding me back?"

Is it the lack of a particular quality, attribute, or skill that sets the speed at which you achieve your goals? Is it a particular attitude or belief that is holding you back? And most important, what could you do immediately to alleviate your key constraints?

Eliminate the Bottlenecks

1. Set clear, measurable goals for sales and profitability. Now ask, "What determines the speed at which I achieve these goals?"

2. Use sentence-completion exercises. Say, "We could double our sales if it weren't for..." and fill in the blank.

3. Identify the major block to achieving your most important goal? How could you remove it?

4. Look within your company for the limiting factors that hold you back. What are the chokepoints in your business?

5. Assess each person in each key position. Are they competent and capable of doing what needs to be done for you to be successful?

6. Once you have identified your key constraint to business success, ask, "*What else* is holding us back?" Keep asking, "What else?" until you get to the real problem.

7. In your own career and personal life, what sets the speed at which you achieve your goals? Look within yourself for the answers.

CHAPTER 17

Reengineer Your Company

The productivity of a work group seems to depend on how the group members see their own goals in relation to the goals of the organization.

—PAUL HERSEY

Your goal should be to build a sleek, efficient, highly profitable business organization with no waste or fat, streamlined to operate smoothly in every respect and in any market. The only question you should ask is, "How am I going to achieve this goal?"

The reengineering process, made famous by Michael Hammer and James Champy in their book *Reengineering the Corporation,* refers to just one thing—simplifying the process of doing business so that it is more streamlined and efficient, faster and more effective, and therefore more profitable.

The Battle Against Complexity

In every part of life, and especially in business and bureaucracy, there is a natural tendency toward complexity. Step by step, even the simplest process becomes more involved, requiring ever more activities to accomplish the same result. Each new step seems logical at the time, but the additional steps gradually increase the cost and decrease the efficiency of the entire process.

The Law of Complexity

Over many years of working with businesses and organizations, I have developed what I call "The Law of Complexity." This law states that "The complexity of a process increases by the square of the number of steps in that process."

Complexity is defined as "the *potential* increase in cost and time and in the number of mistakes that occur in completing any task or finishing any project."

An important part of this definition is the word *potential* with regard to costs, time, and mistakes. It does not mean that a complex process will definitely suffer all the additional costs and delays generally created by adding steps. It simply means that the *probability* will increase dramatically as the complexity increases.

Simple vs. Complex Tasks

This is how the law of complexity works. If there is only one step in a process, the square of one is still *one*. The level of complexity is very low in a single-step activity. The potential costs, time, and mistakes are low as well. For example, if you decide to make a phone call, and you do it yourself, the action is simple and direct. There is virtually no complexity. The number of mistakes you can make is only one, misdialing the number.

Once you add a second step, you have a complexity level of two. The number two squared is *four*. The level of complexity has now jumped from one to four, and the likelihood of mistakes, increased costs, and delays has gone up by 400 percent. An example of this would be if you asked someone else to make a phone call for you to relay a message and get a reply. The room for miscommunication and the probability of missed messages jump dramatically.

Exponential Increases

If you add a third step, the number three squared equals *nine*. The complexity level is now nine in terms of potential costs, delays, and mistakes. For example, let us imagine that you ask someone to ask someone *else* to make a phone call for you, relay a message, and get an answer. The potential for miscommunication, and all the increased costs, delays, and problems that may go along with this confusion have jumped 900 percent from when you thought of making the call yourself.

As you keep adding more steps, the level of complexity begins to increase exponentially. Once you have a process with ten or fifteen steps, the costs, time, and possible mistakes go through the roof and out of sight. This principle explains $3,500 toilet seats in the military and the hundreds of millions of dollars of waste that has to be written off in government projects each year. The complexity levels are so high that it takes years to get something done, the costs are horrendous, and there are usually numerous mistakes.

Reduce the Steps

The key to simplifying and streamlining your work and your business lies in your ability to reduce the number of steps in each process. When you reduce a process by a single step, as in going from five steps (a complexity level of twenty-five) to four steps (a complexity level of sixteen), you reduce the possible costs, delays, and mistakes by a factor of nine! As you reduce steps, you speed up your ability to get results, at lower cost, and with fewer mistakes.

In the process of reengineering, you stop the clock—like calling a "time out!" in a football game—on a particular business activity that has become complex and time-consuming. You then analyze every step involved in the process of doing that job, writing the steps down in order.

Simplify the Process

Once you have made a list of every step, you go through the list, looking for ways to reduce steps wherever you possibly can. You know that even a single step reduction in a process will dramatically reduce the complexity and thereby increase the speed at which the job or task is accomplished.

You act as your own management consultant and ask hard questions, just as you would if you had been hired from the outside. Ask why every single step is being taken. What is its purpose? Why is it being done in this particular way?

The second stage of reengineering is for you to go through the list with the goal of eliminating at least 30 percent of the steps the first time through. This is virtually always achievable, sometimes to the amazement of everyone involved. It just takes a little imagination.

Collapse the Process

Here is an example. Northwest Mutual Life Assurance Company, prior to reengineering the process, required six weeks to approve a life insurance policy application from the field. By the time the approval got back to the agent, the prospective client had often decided to go somewhere else or not to buy the policy at all.

When they analyzed the six-week process, they found that there were twenty-four steps in the approval or disapproval of a life insurance application. Twenty-four different people had to examine some part of the application. But the total amount of time actually spent on each application turned out to be only seventeen minutes.

It turned out that this process had developed over many years as a way of avoiding mistakes in policy approvals. Each time a mistake had been made in the past, another check or control was created to catch the mistake in the future.

The process had obviously become too cumbersome so they decided to reengineer it. The method turned out to be quite simple. They consolidated twenty-three of the twenty-four steps into a single job for a single person, who checked every detail of the policy before sending it to a supervisor. The supervisor simply checked the first person's analysis and gave an approval or disapproval. The answer went back to the field within twenty-four hours. As a result of this new speed of processing, Northwestern Mutual was able to write many hundreds of millions of dollars of additional insurance every year.

Consolidate and Eliminate Steps

In reengineering, you first eliminate every unnecessary step that you possibly can. Next, you look for ways to *consolidate* steps into one job so that more of them can be done by a single person or at the same time, rather than being stretched out.

In some of the small, efficient airlines today, you will often find that the person who checks you in and gives you your ticket is the same person who clears you onto the plane at boarding. Then, you look up and find that he or she is the flight attendant. When you arrive, he or she is busy gathering newspapers and cleaning up for the next flight. At some airlines, each of these jobs is done by a different person. Which airlines do you think are the most profitable and efficient?

Outsource Everything Possible

In your drive for simplification, look for ways to outsource every job that another company can do instead of you. Any function that is not a part of your core business is a candidate for outsourcing, from accounting to computer/Internet maintenance to payroll to printing. Companies that specialize in a particular business function can usually do it cheaper and better than you can anyway.

Delegate Lower-Value Tasks

Delegate any parts of your work that can be done by other people so you can focus on tasks of higher value. Discontinue any activities that don't contribute value to your products, your services, or your customers. Constantly seek ways to reduce the number of steps in your work process.

Habit is a terrible thing. You can become comfortable doing things in a certain way and be reluctant to change. But if you are going to free up your time and resources to do more of those things that your customers really value, you must be absolutely ruthless about consolidating, outsourcing, delegating, and eliminating as many parts of the work as possible.

Root It Out

A step in a work process is very much like crab grass. If you don't root it out completely, it grows again into increased complexity. Sometimes the smartest thing you can do is to stop a particular activity altogether. Eliminate it completely. If it doesn't contribute significant value, or if you wouldn't start it again today, abandon it and invest your time and energy in more important tasks with a higher potential payoff.

Practice *management by responsibility*. Give the complete responsibility to another person to do the job in its entirety so that you can be free of it completely. Look for ways to simplify and reduce complexity.

Find Someone Else to Do It

When you begin your career, you will find yourself doing a great number of tasks. As you rise to positions of greater responsibility, it is natural that you bring these old tasks along, like old friends whose company you have come to enjoy. It is the most natural thing in management to fall back into doing those things you have already mastered, especially under the pressure of deadlines, or when you are feeling impatient.

You have heard the old adage: "If you want something done right, you have to do it yourself." However, that is old-school thinking. Today, the correct response is "If you want something done right, you have to find someone else who can do it almost as well as (or better than) you."

Manage by Exception

Another way to simplify your work is for you to *manage by exception.* Once you have assigned a job to a competent person, require reporting only if there is a deviation from what you have agreed upon. Avoid the tendency to overmanage or to require continuous approvals as the process goes along. Simplify, simplify, simplify.

Make Faster, Better Decisions

Another way to speed up the work process is to make decisions quickly. Don't let them pile up. Don't keep people waiting. Often the failure or reluctance to make a decision acts like a plug in a drain. It stops up the whole process. No one else can do their work while they wait for someone else to decide.

One of the best ways to speed up the process of decision-making is to delegate it to others. Encourage your staff to make decisions based on their own common sense, without referring to you or getting your permission. Whenever they bring you a problem or a question, always ask, "What do *you* think we should do?"

Whatever their answer, within reason, let them do it. You will be amazed at how quickly people grow in decision-making ability and how well their decisions come out. Practice the rule: "If it is not necessary for you to decide, it is necessary for you *not* to decide." This is a great way to simplify your life.

Operate in Real Time

From now on, make it a game to reduce processing time in every area. Think in terms of speed and efficiency. Develop and encourage a "sense of urgency" in everyone around you. Try to operate in "real time" by doing the job the moment it comes up. Work quickly once you get started. Get the job done fast.

Whenever anyone suggests adding an additional step to any job or project, put a halt to it immediately. For the rest of your business career, look for ways to get things done faster and easier by reducing steps and thereby reducing complexity.

Simplify Your Personal Life

Take an inventory of your personal life. Look especially at the areas where you feel overwhelmed with too much to do and too little time. Then make a decision to reengineer your life.

Continually seek out ways to reduce complexity by reducing the number of steps in each process. Look for tasks and activities that you can delegate, downsize, and eliminate.

Meanwhile, resolve to spend more time doing the things that you most enjoy, and which are most important to your success and happiness.

Reengineer Your Company

1. Practice simplification as a way of life. In what areas of work has your life become too complicated, and what can you do to get it back under control?

2. Practice zero-based thinking with every step and every activity. If you were not now doing it this way, would you start doing it this way again today?

3. Take a single complex process or job and make a list of every

step from beginning to end. How could you reduce the number of steps by 30 percent the first time through?

4. What tasks or activities could you delegate to someone who can do them 70 percent as well as you?

5. What parts of your business could you outsource to companies or individuals who specialize in that area?

6. What parts of your work could you eliminate altogether with little or no impact on your bottom line?

7. What parts of your personal life do you need to streamline and simplify? When are you going to do it?

CHAPTER 18

Pump Up Your Profits

Most successful men have not achieved their distinction by having some new talent or opportunity presented to them. They have developed the opportunity that was at hand.

—BRUCE BARTON

There is a truism that 50 percent of advertising is wasted, but no one ever knows for sure which 50 percent it is. As a result, advertising budgets always seem higher than necessary. This problem persists in many areas of many businesses today. Money is being wasted, but no one is exactly sure where and how it is happening.

Low Profits or No Profits

Many companies today are earning low profits or no profits because their costs of doing business are not coordinated with their sales. Many products and services are priced by people who are completely unaware of the real costs involved in bringing those products or services to the market. These mistakes in pricing are then buried in the overall operations and general revenues of the business.

You've heard the saying, "We lose money on every sale, but we make it up on the volume."

In many cases, this is not a joke. It is common for companies to have too many products or services at too many price points, aimed at too many markets and sold in too many different ways. Many of these companies are losing money on the sales of certain products, or making far less than they could be if they knew the true costs of bringing those products or services to market.

Conduct a Profit Analysis on Every Product

One of the most important parts of the Turbostrategy process is for you to conduct a complete profit analysis on each product or service you sell. Very few companies have ever done this. But when you begin applying profit analysis in your company, you can often increase your profits dramatically.

You begin the process of profit analysis by applying the 80/20 Rule to every part of your business. You determine which 20 percent of your products or services account for 80 percent of your sales. Then you determine which products or services account for 80 percent of your profits. You will be surprised to learn that the answers to these two questions are not necessarily the same.

You then analyze your costs and determine the 20 percent of activities that account for 80 percent of your expenses of doing business. You analyze your customers to determine the 20 percent who represent 80 percent of your sales.

High-Volume vs. High-Profit Customers

As you examine these numbers, you will find that, in many cases, your biggest customers are not your most profitable customers, and your biggest selling products or services are not your most profitable ones either. You may find that your costs of doing business with some customers and with some products are so high that it is hardly worth the investment of people and resources. This can only be determined by taking a hard look at the numbers.

When a turnaround specialist takes over a company in trouble, she immediately conducts a profit analysis. She analyzes every product or service to determine quickly which ones are the most profitable, which are the second most profitable, and which are the least profitable.

Once this analysis is complete, the turnaround specialist moves quickly to discontinue, sell off, and close down unprofitable elements of the business. Her sole focus is on cash flow, which comes largely from selling something and getting paid for it quickly.

Focus on Cash Flow

You need to be your own turnaround specialist all the time, and most especially when business slows for any reason. To pump up your profits, you do a complete profit analysis on your business and move immediately to focus the energies of the company on those areas that represent the very best sources of net cash. This process requires that you continuously analyze your business so that you know exactly the profitability of every product and service you sell in comparison with every other product or service you sell, right down to the penny.

Many companies, as they grow, fall into the habit of including more and more expenses such as salaries, rent, telephones, travel, and even advertising under the category of "General and Administrative." Only costs that can be directly attributed to a specific product or service are used for costing purposes. As a result, many costs get "buried" in the bookkeeping, and even the person in charge is not aware of the exact sources and uses of cash.

From Most to Least Profitable

The fact is that, with a little effort, every single product or service can be organized on a scale from the most profitable to the least profitable, both on a per item or per hour basis, and in net dollar amounts. There is always one that is more profitable than any other. There is a second that follows closely behind the first. There is a third and a fourth, and so on. Your job is to determine exactly what they are and in which order.

Determining Profitability

You begin your profit analysis by determining the exact gross sales revenues that you receive from a product or service after all subtractions for defects, returns, breakage, loss, wastage, and bad debts. Take every single deduction so that your gross dollar amount is completely accurate, and you are crystal-clear about the exact amount you are netting from sales.

Once you have an accurate top-line figure, the next step is for you to determine 100 percent of the costs of providing that product or service to the customer. These include the direct costs of producing and delivering the product or service, plus the indirect, variable, semi-variable, and fixed costs that must be allocated to get an accurate number. You must be absolutely, brutally honest with yourself in determining these costs.

Apportion Costs Accurately

You must calculate and deduct a percentage of the labor costs of every person in the organization who has anything to do with the product or service. You should deduct a portion of the rent, the electricity, the telephones, the utilities, and all general administration costs. These are real costs of doing business that must be included for you to get an accurate assessment of that product's profitability.

Now, if you haven't done it already, you deduct a percentage of all costs of advertising, promotion, marketing, labor, commissions, and, especially, your own time investment, and the time investment of other executives, based on your and their hourly rates from each unit of product or service sold.

Calculate the Hourly Rates

People are often confused about the subject of *hourly rate*. The fact is that it costs a company three to six times a person's salary to keep him or her employed. The additional costs are included in benefits provided, the costs of the offices and other facilities a person needs to do his or her job, vacations, pension plan contributions, and the cost of other managers and staff to supervise or support him.

Using a simple calculation, you can divide your annual income by 2,000 hours, the average American work year, to get your hourly rate. For example, if you earn $100,000 per year, divided by 2,000, your hourly rate is equal to $50 per hour. Therefore, every hour you spend on a product or project is costing your company that amount in direct salary cost, plus at least twice that amount in associated or "indirect costs." This is the real figure that must be included to calculate the true profits that the company earns from a product or a customer.

Include the Opportunity Costs

Many small-business owners and managers forget that their labor has a real "opportunity" cost. If it were applied to another task, it could be generating $50, $100, and more per hour. If you spend one hour working on a sale, you must add one hour of your time to the cost of making that sale or deduct the cost of one hour from the profit the company made from that sale.

Many companies find that, because of the demands that some customers place on their executives and staff, the company is actually losing money every time it does business with that particular customer. We call this a "high maintenance" customer. The more time you spend with "high maintenance" customers, the less time you have to spend with other customers who may be more profitable in terms of net dollars to your business.

Rank All Your Products

Now you are ready for the next step, ranking all your products or services, from the most profitable to the least profitable, on a list. What is your number-one, most profitable product, after you have deducted all your possible costs, both direct and indirect?

Often there is little or no relationship between the amount of time and money you spend creating and selling a product and the amount of profit you earn on that product after all costs are deducted. Sometimes your most profitable products, activities, or customers are taken for granted or go unnoticed.

Identify your most profitable and your least profitable customers. What are the common characteristics of each type? How could you structure your business so that you attract and keep more of those customers that represent the most profit for what you sell?

Face the Bitter Truth

You will probably find that fully half of your product and service offerings are generating very little profit or even causing you to lose money with every sale. A turnaround specialist would immediately either raise the prices of the low-profit items or discontinue them altogether. You must do the same.

You can often transform your results and increase your profitability quickly by applying a rigid profit analysis to everything you sell. You could probably discontinue 80 percent of your product or service lines without any great loss. You could then commit 100 percent of your people and resources to the 20 percent of products or services that account for 80 percent of your profits today. Think about what a difference that would make!

Take a *long-term perspective* on your business. Think about your best and most profitable products of today. Then think about your best and most profitable products of yesterday. Based on the trends in your business, what are likely to be your most profitable products and services of tomorrow? Remember: "The best way to predict the future is to create it."

Look Into Yourself

Finally, look at yourself as a business as well. Identify the few things you do that make the greatest contribution to your organization. What activities pay you the highest hourly rate? What are the opportunities of tomorrow for you? What additional skills and competencies could you acquire that would make you even more valuable in the months and years ahead? Whatever they are, the time to start learning them is now. There is no time to waste.

Pump Up Your Profits

1. Do a complete profit analysis on every product and service you offer. Rank them from highest to lowest.

2. Identify the 20 percent of your products that account for 80 percent of your sales. Which are they?

3. Identify the 20 percent of your products and services that account for 80 percent of your profits. Are they the same as your answer to #2?

4. After deducting all direct and indirect costs, which are your most profitable products or services based on cost and return on investment?

5. How much is your time worth on an hourly basis? Build this cost into everything you do to get an accurate measure of costs and profitability.

6. Attribute a percentage of all general and administrative costs to each product or service you sell. This exercise often turns profits into losses.

7. If your company were facing serious financial shortages, which products or services would you focus your energies on, and which would you discontinue? Think about doing it now.

CHAPTER 19

Commit to Continuous Improvement

The quality of a person's life is in direct proportion to their commitment to excellence, regardless of their chosen field of endeavor.

—VINCE LOMBARDI

The quality revolution in America, which started in Japan, has swept across the country and transformed the way we do business. At one time, having a quality product was necessary if you wanted to grow in market share and profitability. Today, you must have a high-quality product if you want to get *into* the market in the first place. Quality today is both expected and demanded by every customer in everything you sell.

The good news is that there are numerous ways you can improve in almost every area of your business. Your job is to look for ways to do things better, cheaper, and faster every day. You must act as if you are

125

being pursued by an aggressive competitor who is determined to put you out of business by satisfying your customers better than you can.

The Quality Revolution

After World War II, Japan was devastated and the economy was in ruins. The first attempts at recovery led to the manufacture of cheap goods for export, especially to America. These early products, which flooded into the U.S. market in the 1950s, were of such poor quality that they were nicknamed "Jap scrap."

In the 1950s, an American management consultant visited Japan to advise them on quality-control methods. The Japanese welcomed his ideas with such enthusiasm that he spent the next few decades there. He changed Japan and the Japanese economy forever.

The Kaizen Method

W. Edwards Deming introduced the concept of continuous improvement, what came to be called the "Kaizen method" of quality improvement, into Japanese manufacturing. This single method enabled the Japanese to evolve in a few years into a nation with a reputation for high-quality manufacturing in virtually every area.

The Japanese word *kaizen* means "continuous betterment." This is sometimes referred to this as the process of "Continuous And Never-Ending Improvement" or CANEI. This approach to business is based on the belief that it is possible to get better at everything you do, continuously, without end.

A New Way of Thinking

When the Kaizen process is introduced, everyone at every level of the business is encouraged to look for ways to do their jobs and produce their products or services better, faster, or cheaper. Management uses suggestion boxes, brainstorming meetings, bonus systems, and constant encouragement to get everyone thinking, all the time, about how to conduct the business in a better way.

Continuous improvement does not require great breakthrough ideas to revolutionize the way business is done, although these breakthroughs occasionally occur. Instead, "line-of-sight" improvements are encouraged in every job. This line-of-sight approach is based on the belief that everyone can see little things they can do to improve their work in their own personal line of sight.

It Starts from the Top

Encourage each person to find ways to do their jobs better, faster, and more easily. Allow them the freedom to experiment with improvements with no fear of criticism if they don't work. Sometimes the greatest improvements occur as the result of a series of small experiments that were not successful.

You should stand back regularly and examine every product, service, and process. How could you improve it in some way? How could you make it better, faster, or cheaper? How could you get the same or better results faster or at a lower cost? Never be satisfied or content with existing quality levels. Always look for ways to improve upon them.

Brainstorm with your team regularly to generate ideas to cut costs, improve quality, increase sales, and boost profits. Encourage everyone to think, all day long, about how they can do their jobs better. Make this commitment to continuous improvement a part of your corporate culture.

Total Quality Management

The total quality management (TQM) movement is based on carefully analyzing every step of every process and then looking for ways to improve continuously in every area. One improvement in a key area can give you a competitive advantage in a tough market.

In a competitive business, if you don't upgrade your quality, your competitors will upgrade theirs and take your business away. The fact is that whatever got you to where you are today is not enough to keep you there. Whatever you are doing today, you will have to be doing it considerably better a year from now if you still want to be in business.

Remember, your competitors are thinking day and night about taking your customers away and putting you out of business. The fastest and best way that they can do this is by offering competitive products at the same price but at a higher level of quality. Your goal is to surpass them in the area of quality improvement before they surpass you.

Benchmark Yourself Against Others

One way to keep on the leading edge of continuous improvement is to benchmark yourself against the very best people and companies in your business. Select a particular function, such as sales, manufacturing, distribution, or customer service, and then determine who excels in the business in that area. Find out what they are doing and copy it the very best way you can. Once you have copied the best-in-class, look for ways to improve and become even better than they are.

Be the Best at What You Do

Set *excellence* as your standard and strive toward it every day. Tell everyone in your company that your goal is to "be the best" in your product or service category. Be extremely demanding in terms of quality standards. Set a high standard for others.

Refuse to allow any product or service to go out the door that is not excellent in every respect. If you hear of a customer who is dissatisfied because of a product defect, you should take it as a personal affront. Immediately apologize to that customer and then do whatever you can to correct the error. Customer satisfaction should be the driving force behind everything you do in your business.

Commit to Excellence

One of the greatest motivators in the world of work is to know that you are working for a company that is committed to excellence. If you could only own one word in the minds and hearts of your prospects and customers, it would be the word "Best!" If everyone in your marketplace referred to you and your offerings as "the best in the business," what kind of difference would that make in your sales and profitability?

With that as your goal, what would you have to do, starting today, to ensure that everyone refers to you as "the best" sometime in the future? What could you do, starting today, to begin this process? What is the first step you should take?

Quality and Profitability

According to the Harvard Profit Impact on Market Strategies (PIMS) studies, a compilation of the financial results of several hundred companies over a twenty-year period, there is a direct relationship between perceived quality and profitability. The higher the perceived quality of your product or service in comparison with that of your competitors, the more profitable your business will be.

For example, if an independent research company were to conduct a poll in your market area, presenting a list of all the companies in your business, and ask "Which of these companies do you feel is the best in this particular industry?" the company that ranked the *highest* in public perception would also turn out to be the most profitable in that sector. The company that was ranked second would turn out to be the second most profitable, and so on.

Here's the question: If such a survey were done among potential customers for what you sell, where do you feel your company would rank in such a comparison? Would you be ranked as "the best," or somewhere lower? What could you do to move *higher* in the rankings? What one step could you take immediately?

How Do Customers Define Quality?

When Gordon Bethune took over troubled Continental Airlines, he ordered a study to determine how flyers defined *quality* and what they wanted most. The overwhelming answer was "on-time arrivals and departures." This goal became his central focus for the next three years.

And it worked. Continental's punctuality improved dramatically. As on-time arrivals and departures got better and better, sales, profitability, customer satisfaction, employee morale, and stock price all improved dramatically. By focusing on "being the best" in a specific area that was of paramount importance to customers, Continental became one of the most impressive business turnarounds of the 1990s.

What Do Customers Want?

Quality is not objective, existing by itself, nor is it defined by the company. It is emotional and subjective, and it is defined by your customers. Quality is what *they* say it is. To paraphrase a famous legal opinion, "I can't define it exactly, but I know what it is when I see it."

Customers define quality in two parts. First is the product or service itself. A quality product or service is something that does what it is supposed to do. It does what the customer was promised when she bought it, and continues to do it.

The second part of quality, from the customer's viewpoint, is the manner in which the product is sold, serviced, and delivered. This personal or emotional component is often more important than the product or service itself. In one study, the researchers found that 68 percent of customer defections to the competition were not product, price, or capability determined. Instead, the primary reason for changing was a perceived indifference on the part of someone in the selling organization.

Rank Yourself Against Your Competitors

Give yourself a grade on a scale of one or ten with regard to the quality of your product or service in comparison with your competitors. Be honest with yourself. Ask everybody in the office to contribute his or her opinions as well. Ask your best customers how they would rate you against the other companies in your business. Whatever score you finally agree on, use that number as your *baseline* for improvement.

Once you have an estimate of your quality ranking, your goal should be to improve it by *one* grade. For example, if on a scale of one to ten you give yourself a score of *seven*, your aim will be to work yourself up to an *eight*. Once you have worked yourself up to an eight, your goal will be to work yourself up to a *nine*, and so on until you reach a *ten* ranking. Your long-term goal is for customers to refer to you as "the best in the business."

Your Personal Quality Rating

The same principle of continuous improvement applies to you personally as well. Identify the most important thing you do for your business and your customers. Give yourself a grade in that area from one to ten. Ask your coworkers, your boss and your customers how they would rate you in that area. Then commit yourself to doing whatever you have to do to increase your ranking by one grade at a time until you achieve absolute excellence in your key skill areas.

Practice the Kaizen method of *continuous betterment*, and the CANEI method of *continuous and never-ending improvement* in everything you do. Never be satisfied with your current level of performance. Every day, in every way, you should look for ways to do your job even better than the day before. Whatever got you to where you are today is not enough to keep you there. Continually raise the bar on yourself. Your life only gets better when you do.

Commit to Continuous Improvement

1. How do your customers define quality? What is most important to them in choosing your product or service?

2. How do you rank against your competitors on a scale of one to ten? How could you improve your ranking immediately?

3. Set up a reward system in your company for suggestions and ideas to improve quality and achieve greater customer satisfaction.

4. Do you have quality and performance standards for people, products, and activities in your company? Does everyone know what they are?

5. What company do you think is the best in your business, the most respected and profitable? How could you benchmark yourself against them?

6. What one step could you take immediately to improve customer satisfaction with your company?

7. What could you do personally to upgrade and improve the quality of your performance in the most important things you do in your job?

CHAPTER 20

Concentrate on the Core

And herein lies the secret of true power. Learn, by constant practice, how to husband your resources, and concentrate them, at any given moment, upon a given point.

—JAMES ALLEN

Almost every business begins with a single idea for a single product or service in the minds of one or two people. Over time, with experience, this core product changes and crystallizes. If the product and the market are right, the company turns the corner and begins to grow in sales and profitability. It does more and more of what it does well and eventually pulls ahead of its competition.

This is your core business. This is what you do best. This is what your customers like the most and what is most profitable for you. This product or service is the foundation of your enterprise. It is what you are known for and what you are most capable of delivering in an excellent fashion.

Define Your Core Business

What is your core business? If everything else were stripped away, what would be left at your core? What is the last product or service you would stop producing or offering?

Whatever it is, the natural tendency of most people is to take their core business, their critical products or services, for granted. Because you are good in that area, because it is a cash cow for you, you begin to assume it will always be there. You then turn your attention to other products or services where you may have limited experience, where you may not be very good at all. This happens to almost every company, more often during periods of growth and profitability in your core business. It can be a real danger.

Watch Your Core Business

The more you get away from your core business, the more time and energy you will invest in things that are "non-core." You will use your core business to generate the funds that you then invest in areas that turn out to be less and less profitable. If you are not careful, someone can come along and steal your core business away from you. Then you will be in serious trouble.

Never let your core business out of your sight. In *Profit from the Core*, Chris Zook and James Allen explain the nature and importance of the core business in detail. After working with hundreds of corporations, Zook and Allen concluded that the best and smartest strategy for a company in the face of competitive pressures or shrinking markets is to get back to its core and stay there.

Concentrate Your Attention

Apply the 80/20 Rule continuously to every part of your business. Discipline yourself to identify and focus on the 20 percent of your products or services that account for 80 percent of your sales and profits.

Determine the 20 percent of your products and services that account for 80 percent of your sales volume. Determine the 20 percent of your customers that purchase 80 percent of your products and services. Determine the 20 percent of people in your business who generate 80 percent of your results.

Identify the 20 percent of opportunities available to you today that can be responsible for 80 percent of your sales and revenues in the years ahead. These will almost always be extensions of your current business, your core competencies, and your areas of excellence. Your choice of the opportunities available to you largely determines the future of your business. What are they?

Focus on Value

What are the 20 percent of your work activities that account for 80 percent of your personal value and your contribution to your company? If you just doubled the amount of time you spend on the 20 percent of your high-value tasks, and discontinued the 80 percent of low-value/no-value tasks that you do, you could become one of the most productive people in your company. These are your core tasks.

What are the 20 percent of problems, aggravations, and irritations that account for 80 percent of your headaches in your work? Who are the most difficult people, customers, or situations that you have to deal with each day? What can you do today to minimize or eliminate them?

Based on this 80/20 analysis, what steps can you take immediately to improve, increase, and strengthen your core products, services, customers, and activities? What should you do first?

Where Do You Excel?

In what areas of your products and services are you, or could you be, *better* than 95 percent of your competition? This is where your greatest opportunities for sales, growth, and profitability will lie. This is where you should dedicate most of your energies and attention.

The biggest mistake you can make in business is to deviate too far from your core business, from what you do really well. As my friend Charlie Jones says, "Side roads are *slide* roads."

Whenever you experience problems with sales or profitability, you should get back to your core business. You should do more of what you do best and do it better. Keep focused on those products, services, and activities that generate the highest and most predictable profits. Only when you have fully developed and exploited every possible opportunity to expand your core business should you expand or digress into untested business areas.

Your Citadel Strategy

In ancient times, walled cities were built to protect the citizens against marauding tribes and armies. As the city grew, additional concentric circles of defensive walls were built to enclose and protect ever-greater numbers of citizens. The cities came to resemble dartboards with rings surrounding a bull's-eye.

If the city was attacked by an enemy army, the citizenry withdrew behind the outer ring of walls and defended themselves. If the outer wall was breached, the defenders withdrew to the next wall. If that wall was breached, they withdrew to the next wall, and so on, until they were forced back into the most heavily defended part of the city, the citadel. The citadel was the key to the survival of the kingdom. As long as it held, the city could be saved. The enemy could be beaten back and the kingdom rebuilt.

The citadel contained all the treasures of the city and was designed to accommodate the king, the top army officers, the leading citizens, and sufficient soldiers to sustain a prolonged siege. With adequate reserves, the city could survive until a neighboring kingdom sent an army to relieve the defenders.

Define Your Citadel

In your business, you have products, services, and activities that are peripheral to your business—the *outer* walls of sales and revenues—and you have products and services that are central—your c*itadel* business activities that represent the major sources of your profits.

Your core business can be thought of as your "citadel." It represents the product or service lines that are vital for your survival. They must be protected at all costs. As long as you remain strong in these areas, you can withstand market fluctuations and sales declines. You must therefore guard and protect them against all competitors.

Determine Your Core Products and Customers

As a matter of business policy, you should develop a "citadel strategy" for your business, especially in times of contracting markets, reduced profitability, and declining cash flow. This strategy should include the setting aside of reserves to carry you over, based on a "worst-case" scenario.

You should always have a citadel strategy on hand. You should analyze and determine your most valuable, important, and profitable products and guard them carefully. When your business takes a dip and you have to defend and protect your ability to survive, be prepared to withdraw to your citadel of key products and services.

Advance Planning

In times of turbulence, rapid change, slowing sales, or disrupted markets, you must develop such a strategy *in advance*, to assure the survival and long-term success of your business. This is a fallback strategy that you have fully prepared in the event of unexpected reverses in the marketplace. Never rely on luck or on an early turnaround to a market trend. Prepare for the worst.

This citadel is your core business. What is it? Whatever it is, practice "scenario planning" on a regular basis. Ask yourself, "What is the worst thing that could possibly happen in my market today?"

Whatever your answer is to that question, begin making provisions today to assure that you will be able to survive should the worst occur.

Play Down the Board

The very best leaders think several moves ahead on the chessboard of business and attempt to anticipate the various moves that might be made against them. They then make provisions in terms of cash reserves, alternate strategies, secured customers and markets, and new product or service offerings to make sure that the worst never occurs. You should do the same.

Develop a citadel strategy for your business today. Be like Napoleon, who was once asked if he believed in luck. He said, "Yes, I believe in luck. And I believe that it will always be bad luck and that I will be the victim of it. I therefore plan accordingly."

Your Personal Citadel Strategy

As an individual, you must be clear about your personal core competencies as well. How could you improve in each one of them? What core competencies will you need to lead your field in the years ahead? What is your plan to acquire the core competencies of tomorrow?

Concentrate on the Core

1. What is your core business? What products and services are most responsible for your success today?

2. What are your core competencies? What is it that your company does extremely well?

3. What are the worst possible things that could happen to your business in the next year? What are your plans to deal with them should they occur?

4. What are your non-core products, services, or activities? What would happen if you discontinued them entirely?

5. Who are your core customers, and what are you doing to assure that they never leave you?

6. Who are your core people, the ones who are most important for the survival and growth of your business? What is your strategy to keep them?

7. What are your core functions? What are the things you do that are central to your job? What activities are peripheral?

CHAPTER 21

Focus on Results

He who every morning plans the transactions of the day and follows out that plan, carries a thread that will guide him through the labyrinth of the most busy life.

—VICTOR HUGO

The great football coach Vince Lombardi, once said, "Winning isn't everything, but wanting to win is."

By the same token, results are not the only thing, but they are everything in business. They are the only true measure of personal ability and corporate effectiveness.

All customers really care about is, "Did I get the results that you promised when I bought this product or service from you?" They have no sympathy whatever for your problems with people, products, processes, delivery systems, or anything else. All your customers care about is results.

Four Key Questions

When considering buying a product or service, customers have four questions that must be answered before going ahead:

1. What does it cost?

2. What do I get for the money?

3. How fast do I get the benefits you promise?

4. How sure can I be that I will get those benefits?

Whichever company or salesperson answers these questions most convincingly wins the sale.

Deliver on Your Promises

Business success is in direct proportion to how consistently and dependably you deliver on your promises. Sales and growth are determined by how reliably your product or service delivers the results that customers pay for. In evaluating your products and services, you must always ask, "What results or benefits do my customers expect of my product or service?" and "How consistently do my customers get those results and benefits when they buy my products or services?" This is the true definition of "quality."

Quality can be defined as "the percentage of times that your product or service does what you say it will do and continues to do it."

A quality rating of 100 percent, or perfect, means that what you sell *always* delivers on your promises. A quality rating of 90 percent means that your product gets the desired or promised results nine out of ten times.

Little Things Mean a Lot

Federal Express has determined that if its quality rating were 99.90 percent, it would make mistakes in the delivery of 44,000 envelopes a day.

At 99.90 percent quality, Federal Express would collapse under its own weight of confusion. That is how important quality is in a business.

Your personal success is also determined by how consistently and dependably you perform and deliver on your responsibilities and promises. You should continually ask yourself, "What results are expected of me?"

Your level of effectiveness is always defined by *others*, by what they need from you. Leaders are always asking, "What does this situation need from me?" Once they are clear, they concentrate their energies in those areas.

Ask yourself, "Of all the results I can accomplish, what are the most valuable and important in terms of my rewards and my future?"

Improving Your Ability to Get Results

Here are seven of the best questions you can ask and answer to improve your ability to get results:

- "Why am I on the payroll?" What exactly have you been hired to accomplish? Make sure that what you are doing every day is the answer to this question.

- "What are my highest-value tasks and activities?" Of all the things that you could be doing during the day, what are the activities you engage in that contribute the greatest value to yourself and your company?

- "What are my key result areas?" What are the core competencies and key tasks that you must absolutely, positively do in an excellent fashion to produce the most important and valued results expected of you? Resolve today to become a "do-it-to-yourself-project," to see yourself as a continuous improvement project for which you are responsible. For the rest of your career, dedicate yourself to continually learning and improving in those areas where top performance is most vital to your success. Getting *better* at your key tasks is one of the best time-saving techniques of all.

■ "What can I, and only I, do that, if done well, will make a real difference?" There is always something that only you can do that can make a significant difference to your life and your work. If you don't do it, it won't get done. No one else will do it for you. But if you do it, and you do it well, it can make a significant difference. What is it?

■ "What one skill, if I developed it and did it in an excellent fashion, would have the greatest positive impact on my career?" There is always one skill that, if you developed it and did it well, would have a greater and more positive impact on your career than any other single skill. Your job is to identify that skill and then put your whole heart into becoming absolutely excellent in that area, whatever it is.

■ "What one result, if I achieved it consistently for my customers, would most satisfy those customers and bring me the greatest number of additional customers?" What must your customers be absolutely convinced they will receive from you in order to encourage them to buy your product or service and to recommend it to their friends? How could you improve your quality and service in that area?

■ The final question for personal success is this: "What is the most valuable use of my time right now?" Use this question as your guiding star throughout the day. Keep asking, "What is the most valuable use of my time, right now?" Whatever your answer is to that question is what you should be doing at this particular moment.

Focus all your energies on doing, learning, and practicing those few skills and getting those key results that are valued the most and that make the greatest difference in your work.

All Day Long

If you could only perform one task all day long, what one thing could you do that would contribute more value to your life and work than any other single task or activity? Whatever your answer, put *mastery* of that task at the top of your list of priorities. Dedicate yourself to getting better and better doing the one thing that can make more of a difference than anything else. This is the key to getting superb results at every stage of your life and career.

Seven Steps to Personal Performance

There are seven steps you can take every day to increase your productivity, performance, and output. These seven steps, practiced until they become ingrained habits of thought and action, will enable you to double your productivity, increase your income, and move ahead faster than almost any other things you can do.

Step 1: Set clear, specific, written goals for each important area of your life. Make them measurable and time-bounded, with deadlines and subdeadlines. Make plans for their accomplishment and work on your key goals every day.

Step 2: Think on paper. Make a list of activities for each day before you begin. The best time to make a list is the night before, the last thing before you end the workday, or before you go to bed at night. This allows your subconscious mind to work on your list as you sleep, often giving you ideas and insights for greater accomplishment when you wake up.

Step 3: Set priorities on your list before you begin. Apply the 80/20 Rule and select the top 20 percent of your tasks to work on.

Use the ABCDE Method as well. Go over your list and write an A next to your most important tasks. Write a B next to your second most important tasks. Write a C next to your unimportant tasks. Write a D next to tasks that you can *delegate*, and an E next to tasks that you can *eliminate*. Do this before you begin working.

If you have more than one A task, organize them as A-1, A-2, A-3, and so on. Do the same with your B tasks. The rule is that you never do a B or C task if there is an A task that has not been completed.

Step 4: Practice *creative procrastination* on your list and in your work. Since you are never going to be able to do everything on your list, you are going to have to procrastinate on some tasks. Decide in advance to procrastinate on those tasks of little value or importance. Otherwise, you will *unconsciously* find yourself procrastinating on tasks that can make a real difference in your life.

Step 5: Select your most important task, your "A-1," and discipline yourself to start on that job first thing when you begin work. This task is often worth more than many, if not all, of the other items on your list.

Step 6: Practice *single-handling* with your most important task. Once you have started work on it, resolve to work at it non-stop until it is complete. Concentrate 100 percent on the one job that represents the most valuable use of your time. Discipline yourself to persist without diversion or distraction until it is done.

 Step 7: Develop a *sense of urgency*, a bias for action. Move quickly at your work and throughout the day. Pick up the pace. Develop a faster tempo in everything you do. Get going and keep going quickly.

The faster you move, the more work you get done, and the better you feel. The more you do, the faster you learn, and the better you get. The faster you move, the better you get, and the more you get done, the greater the contribution you make will be, the more you will get paid, and the faster you will be promoted. By moving faster, you will put your whole life and career onto the fast track.

Conclusion

There are many great ideas for personal and business improvement. In this book, we have covered twenty-one concepts for improving performance, increasing sales, cutting costs, and boosting profits. These are key concepts that you should review continuously if you want to be the best you can be personally, and if you want to run the most profitable and successful business possible.

Once more here are the twenty-one key ideas in the TurboStrategy process:

1. **Start Where You Are**: Do a complete and honest analysis of your business as it is today, including the current status of your sales, revenues, profitability, and the market situation around you.

2. **Draw a Line Under the Past:** Apply zero-based thinking to every part of your business. If you were not doing it today, *knowing what you now know*, would you get into it again today?

3. **Conduct a Basic Business Analysis:** Examine your products, services, processes, and activities as if you were looking at them for the first time. Be prepared to ask yourself the "brutal questions" about each one of them.

4. **Decide Exactly What You Want:** Set clear, written, measurable goals and objectives for yourself in each part of your business.

5. **Design Your Ideal Future:** Project forward three to five years and imagine that your business were ideal in every respect. What would it look like? What could you do, starting today, to turn that future vision into a current reality?

6. **Create a Mission Statement:** Decide exactly what it is you want to accomplish for others with your business. Make it measurable. Make it exciting. Share it with everyone.

7. **Reinvent Your Organization:** Imagine starting your business or career over again today with your present knowledge and experience. What would you do differently?

8. **Select the Right People:** Ninety-five percent of your success in business will be determined by the people you choose to work with and for. Take the time to make good personnel decisions.

9. **Market More Effectively:** Think through every part of your marketing strategy by applying the four principles of specialization, differentiation, segmentation, and concentration to every product and service.

10. **Analyze Your Competition:** Decide exactly who you are

competing against and why it is that your prospective customers prefer to buy from them. How could you offset this perceived advantage?

11. **Do It Better, Faster, Cheaper:** Continuously seek ways to serve and satisfy your customer in a fashion superior to that of any one else in your market. Never stop raising the bar on yourself.

12. **Change Your Marketing Mix:** Imagine being your own management consultant and asking yourself hard questions about the appropriateness of your product, price, place, and promotion in today's market.

13. **Position Your Company for Success:** Determine how you want to be thought about and talked about by your customers and prospective customers. What are the very best words they could use to describe you?

14. **Develop Strategic Business Units:** Divide your products and services into one of four categories: cash cows, stars, question marks, and dogs. Make one person responsible for sales and profitability for each product or group of products.

15. **Sell More Effectively:** Focus single-mindedly on upgrading the quality of your sales effort. Hire more selectively, train more thoroughly, and manage more professionally. Sales are the lifeblood of the business.

16. **Eliminate the Bottlenecks:** Identify the factors that determine how fast you achieve your goals of sales and profitability. Concentrate on alleviating these bottlenecks in every part of your business.

17. **Reengineer Your Company:** Constantly seek ways to streamline and simplify the process of producing and selling your products and services. Learn to delegate, out-

source, downsize, and eliminate the complexity of every-thing you do.

18. **Pump up Your Profits:** Evaluate every product and service to determine exactly how much net profit you are actually earning from each item you sell. Resolve to discontinue products and services that are not as profitable as others, and channel more resources into those products that are the mainstays of your business.

19. **Commit to Continuous Improvement:** Install the Kaizen process of "continuous betterment" into your company. Find out how your customer defines "quality" and then strive to exceed expectations.

20. **Concentrate on the Core:** Identify the most important products and services you offer, and then focus on getting better and better selling more and more of them. Probably 80 percent of the market potential for your core products has not yet been tapped.

21. **Focus on Results:** Concentrate your best energies and resources on getting the most important results possible for your company. Set priorities in every area and then work single-mindedly to complete the few tasks that are more valuable than everything else put together.

The most important part of the Turbostrategy is not what you learn, but the actions you take and how quickly you take those actions. There is a direct relationship between how fast you move on a new idea and how likely it is that you will ever move on a new idea. Resolve today to become intensely action-oriented for the rest of your career. Just do it!

Bibliography

Adizes, Ichak. *The Pursuit of Prime: Maximize Your Company's Success with the Adizes Program*, Knowledge Exchange, 1997.

Beatty, Jack. *The World According to Peter Drucker*, New York: Bantam, 1999.

Beckwith, Harry. *The Invisible Touch: The Four Keys to Modern Marketing*, New York: Warner Books, 2000.

Bennis, Warren. *On Becoming a Leader*, New York: Perseus Publishing, 1994.

Bennis, Warren, and Burt Nanus. *Leaders: Strategies for Taking Charge*, New York: HarperBusiness, 1997.

Bossidy, Larry, Ram Charan, and Charles Burck. *Execution: The Discipline of Getting Things Done*, New York: Crown Business, 2002.

Buckingham, Marcus, and Donald O. Clifton. *Now, Discover Your Strengths*, New York: Free Press, 2001.

Caplan, Robert S., and David P. Norton. *The Balanced Scorecard: Translating Strategy Into Action*, Boston: Harvard Business School Press, 1996.

Christensen, Clayton M. *The Innovator's Dilemma: When New Technologies Cause Great Firms to Fail*, Boston: Harvard Business School Press, 1997.

Cialdini, Robert B. *Influence,* New York: Morrow, 1993.

Collins, James C., and Jerry I. Porras. *Built to Last: Successful Habits of Visionary Companies,* New York: HarperBusiness, 2002.

Collins, Jim. *Good to Great: Why Some Companies Make the Leap— And Others Don't,* New York: HarperBusiness, 2001.

Cranier, Stuart, et al. *Key Management Ideas: Thinking That Changed the Management World*, Financial Times Management, 1996.

Crosby, Philip B. *Quality Is Free: The Art of Making Quality Certain.* New York: McGraw-Hill, 1979.

Drucker, Peter. *The Effective Executive*, rev. ed., New York: Harper-Business, 2002.

Drucker, Peter. *The Practice of Management*, New York: HarperBusiness, 1993.

Drucker, Peter. *Managing for Results: Economic Tasks and Risk-Taking Decisions*, New York: HarperBusiness, 1993.

Drucker, Peter. *The Age of Discontinuity: Guidelines to Our Changing Society*, New York: HarperCollins, 1984.

Drucker, Peter. *Innovation and Entrepreneurship*, New York: Harper-Business, 1999.

Drucker, Peter. *Managing for the Future*, New York: Dutton, 1992.

Drucker, Peter. *Managing in Turbulent Times*, New York: HarperBusiness, 1993.

Drucker, Peter. *Managing the Nonprofit Organization: Principles and Practices*, New York: HarperBusiness, 1992.

Drucker, Peter. *Management: Tasks, Responsibilities, Practices*, New York: HarperBusiness, 1993.

Drucker, Peter. *The New Realities: in Government and Politics/in Economics and business/and World View*, New York: HarperBusiness, 1994.

Drucker, Peter. *Managing in a Time of Great Change*, New York: Plume, 1995.

Gilmore, James H., and B. Joseph Pine II. *The Experience Economy*, Boston: Harvard Business School Press, 1999.

Goldratt, Eliyahu, and Jeff Cox. *The Goal*, Great Barrington, MA: North River Press, 1992.

Grove, Andrew S. *High Output Management*, New York: Vintage, 1995.

Hamel, Gary, and C. K. Prahalad. *Competing for the Future*, Boston: Harvard Business School Press, 1994.

Hammer, Michael, and James Champy. *Reengineering the Corporation: A Manifesto for Business Revolution.* New York: HarperBusiness, 2001.

Heller, Robert. *Business Masterminds: Roads to Success*, London: Dorling-Kindersley, 2001.

Kouzes, James M., and Barry Z. Posner. *The Leadership Challenge*, 3/e, San Francisco: Jossey-Bass, 2002.

Levitt, Theodore. *The Marketing Imagination,* rev. ed., New York: Free Press, 1986.

Maxwell, John C. *The 21 Irrefutable Laws of Leadership*, Nashville: Thomas Nelson, 1998.

McKain, Scott. *All Business Is Show Business: Strategies for Earning Standing Ovations from Your Customers*, Rutledge Hill Press, 2002.

McKay, Harvey. *Swim With the Sharks Without Being Eaten Alive: Outsell, Outmanage, Outmotivate, and Outnegotiate Your Competition,* New York: Morrow, 1988.

Montoya, Peter, et al. *The Personal Branding Phenomenon,* Peter Montoya and Tim Vandehey, publishers, 2002.

Morrisey, George L. *Creating Your Future: Personal Strategic Planning for Professionals,* San Francisco: Berrett-Koehler, 1992.

Peppers, Don, and Martha Rogers. *The One to One Future: Building Relationships One Customer at a Time,* New York: Doubleday Currency, 1997.

Peters, Tom, and Robert H. Waterman, Jr. *In Search of Excellence: Lessons from America's Best-Run Companies,* New York: Warner Books, 1988.

Porter, Michael. *Competitive Advantage: Creating and Sustaining Superior Performance,* New York: Free Press, 1998.

Senge, Peter. *The Fifth Discipline: The Art and Practice of the Learning Organization,* New York: Doubleday Currency, 1994.

Ries, Al, and Jack Trout. *Positioning: The Battle for Your Mind,* 20th anniversary ed. New York: McGraw-Hill, 2001.

Ries, Al, and Jack Trout. *Marketing Warfare,* New York: McGraw-Hill, 1997.

Slywotzky, Adrian J., and David J. Morrison. *Profit Patterns: 30 Ways to Anticipate and Profit from Strategic Forces Reshaping Your Business,* New York: Random House, 1999.

Tracy, Brian. *The 100 Absolutely Unbreakable Laws of Business Success,* San Francisco: Berrett-Koehler, 2002.

Tracy, Brian. *Focal Point: A Proven System to Simplify Your Life, Double Your Productivity, and Achieve All Your Goals,* New York: AMACOM—American Management Association, 2001.

Tracy, Brian. *Victory! Applying the Proven Principles of Military Strategy to Achieve Greater Success in Your Business and Personal Life*, New York: AMACOM—American Management Association, 2002.

Tracy, Brian. *Create Your Own Future: How to Master the 12 Critical Factors of Unlimited Success*, New York: Wiley, 2002.

Tracy, Brian. *Goals! How to Get Everything You WantFaster Than You Ever Thought Possible*, San Francisco: Berrett-Koehler, 2003.

Tracy, Brian. *Maximum Achievement: Strategies and Skills That Will Unlock Your Hidden Powers to Succeed*, New York: Fireside, 1995.

Tracy, Brian. *Advanced Selling Strategies: The Proven System of Sales Ideas, Methods, and Techniques Used by Top Salespeople*, New York: Fireside,1996.

Tracy, Brian. *Eat That Frog! 21 Great Ways to Stop Procrastinating and Get More Done in Less Time,* San Francisco: Berrett-Koehler, 2001.

Tracy, Brian. *Many Miles to Go: A Modern Parable for Business Success*, Entrepreneur Media, Inc., 2003.

Treacy, Michael, and Fred Wiersma. *The Discipline of Market Leaders: Choose Your Customers, Narrow Your Focus, Dominate Your Market,* Reading, MA: Addison-Wesley, 1997.

Trout, Jack, and Steve Rivkin. *The Power of Simplicity: A Management Guide to Cutting Through the Nonsense and Doing Things Right*, New York: McGraw-Hill, 2000.

Uris, Auren. *101 of the Greatest Ideas in Management*, New York: Wiley 1987.

Watson, Thomas J., Jr. *A Business and Its Beliefs: The Ideas that Helped Build IBM.* New York: McGraw-Hill, 1963.

Welch, Jack, with John A. Byrne. *Jack: Straight from the Heart*, New York: Warner Books, 2001.

Zook, Chris, and James Allen. *Profit from the Core,* Boston: Harvard Business School Press, 2001.

The TurboStrategy Process

The ideas and concepts described in this book are drawn from my twenty-five years of strategic planning and work with more than 500 companies in the United States, Canada, and twenty-three foreign countries.

In my TurboStrategy process, I spend two or three days working with my clients to crystallize these ideas into a blueprint and a plan of action.

When you apply these concepts to your business, you will develop greater clarity and commitment to your values, vision, mission, purpose, and goals. You will learn how to identify your key result areas and determine your competitive advantages, both existing and potential.

These techniques will help you to analyze your company, inside and out, and decide upon new goals, plans, activities, measures of performance, and responsibilities.

As the result of this TurboStrategy process, you will be able to simplify and streamline your operations, increase sales, revenues, and cash flow, cut costs, and boost your profits—sometimes overnight.

You will achieve new breakthroughs regarding your products, services, customers, markets, and future opportunities.

You will learn to practice the three R's of business success in every area of your business. First, you will continuously *reevaluate* every product, every service and activity, and every person who works in your company.

Second, you will *refocus* your time and resources toward doing more of those things that contribute the highest levels of sales and profitability.

Third, you will *regain control* over your business so you can guide and steer it more effectively in our current economy.

These TurboStrategy ideas are tailored and customized to your unique situation. They are modified to fit your business, your products and services, your customers and markets, your people and processes. The application of these ideas is different for every company.

The Three Steps
There are basically three steps in my TurboStrategy process. They are Pre-work, Course work, and Implementation.

In the pre-work, each participant is required to complete a detailed analysis of the existing business and its operations. A copy of this pre-work is returned to me to enable me to tailor our strategy work together so that is very specific to your current business.

In the two-day intensive strategic planning process, we thoroughly evaluate your business; determine your guiding values, vision, mission, purpose, and goals for the next one to three years; and develop a blueprint for action.

We study each product and service area as it relates to the current market, the competition, and the future. We decide on your marketing, sales, and promotional strategy to generate increased sales, income, and cash flow.

We examine the critical issues, both inside and outside the company, that affect success and growth. We make decisions about what needs to change and how these changes can best be made.

Finally, we reduce the entire planning process to specific action commitments and responsibilities, complete with measurements and timelines.

Each participant emerges from the TurboStrategy session with greater clarity and direction, ready to take action and get better results. Afterwards, I summarize the results and decisions of the session for evaluation and review and to serve as a guide for the future.

We provide all of the written materials necessary to assure the maximum value and effectiveness of the process. I remain available to you as an advisor, consultant, and assistant to ensure the implementation of the strategy of the strategic plan throughout the organization.

This program is conducted away from the office in a private setting where there are no interruptions. It is extraordinarily effective and can change the future of your business.

If you are interested in having me come into your company and work with you and your key executives, please call me at 1-800-542-4252 (ext. 17) and speak with our vice president, Victor Risling. I am looking forward to hearing from you.

The TurboCoaching Process

This intensive one-year program is ideal for ambitious, successful men and women who want to achieve better results and greater balance in their lives.

If you are already earning more than $100,000 per year and if you have a large degree of control over your time, in four full days with me in San Diego—one day every three months—you will learn how to double your productivity and income and double your time off with your family at the same time.

Every ninety days, you work with me and an elite group of successful entrepreneurs, self-employed professionals, and top salespeople for an entire day. During this time together, you form a "mastermind alliance" from which you gain ideas and insights that you can apply immediately to your work and personal life.

The TurboCoaching process is based on four areas of effectiveness: **Clarification, Simplification, Maximization, and Multiplication**. You learn a series of methods and strategies to incorporate these principles into everything you do.

> **Clarification**: You learn how to develop absolute clarity about who you really are and what you really want in each of seven key areas of life. You determine your values, vision, mission, purpose, and goals for yourself, your family, and your work.

> **Simplification**: You learn how to dramatically simplify your life, getting rid of all the little tasks and activities that contribute little to the achievement of your real goals of high income, excellent family relationships, superb health and fitness, and financial independence. You learn how to streamline, delegate, outsource, minimize, and eliminate all those activities that are of little value.

> **Maximization:** You learn how to get the very most out of yourself by implementing the best time and personal management tools and techniques. You learn how to get more done in less time, how to increase your income rapidly, and how to have even more time for your personal life.

> **Multiplication**: You learn how to leverage your special strengths to accomplish vastly more than you could by relying on your own efforts and resources. You learn how to use other people's money, other people's efforts, other people's ideas, and other people's customers and contacts to increase your personal productivity and earn more money.

This TurboCoaching program is called *Focal Point Advanced Coaching and Mentoring.* Brian Tracy gives it personally four times each year in San Diego. Each session includes complete pre-work, detailed exercises and instruction, all materials, plus meals and refreshments during the day. At the end of each session, you emerge with a complete blueprint for the next ninety days.

If you are interested in attending this program, visit our Web site at briantracy.com, or phone our vice president, Victor Risling at 1-800-542-4252 (ext. 17) to request an application form or more information. We look forward to hearing from you.

Index

About the Author

Brian Tracy is one of America's top business speakers, a best-selling author, and one of the leading consultants and trainers on personal and professional development in the world today. He has started, built, managed, or turned around twenty-two different businesses in diverse industries. Brian addresses 250,000 people each year on subjects ranging from Personal Success and Leadership to Managerial Effectiveness, Creativity, and Sales. He has written thirty books, including *Focal Point* (AMA-COM), *Maximum Achievement*, and *The 100 Absolutely Unbreakable Laws of Business Success*, and has produced more than 300 audio and video learning programs. Much of his work has been translated into other languages and is being used in thirty-five countries.

Brian has consulted with more than 500 companies—IBM, McDonnell Douglas, and The Million Dollar Round Table among them—and has trained more than 2,000,000 people personally. His ideas are proven, practical, and fast-acting. His readers and seminar participants learn a series of techniques and strategies that they can use immediately to get better results in their lives and careers.